THE WORLD'S EPOCH-MAKERS

BUDDHA AND BUDDHISM

THE WORLD'S EPOCH-MAKERS

BUDDHA AND BUDDHISM

BY

Arthur Lillie

"Buddhism in Christendom" "The Popular Life of Buddha"
etc. etc.

"O God in the form of Mercy!"

Ancient Stone Inscription, Gaya

GYAN

Published by

GYAN

Gyan Publishing House
5, Ansari Road
Daryaganj, New Delhi-110002
Phone: 011-47034999, 9811692060
E-mail: books@gyanbooks.com

Distribution Network
gyanbooks.com
India, USA, Canada, UK, Australia, France

ISBN : 978-81-212-3161-9 (PB)
First Published, 1900

2nd Impression 2020

Printed at: Gyan Press, Delhi.

Buddha and Buddhism
Author: Arthur Lillie

THE WORLD'S EPOCH-MAKERS

Buddha and Buddhism

By

Arthur Lillie

Author of
"Buddhism in Christendom" "The Popular Life of Buddha"
etc. etc.

"O God in the form of Mercy!"

Ancient Stone Inscription, Gâyâ

New York. Charles Scribner's Sons

1900

PREFACE

THE Queen has in her possession a piece of ivory or bone little valued by her white-faced subjects, but immensely esteemed by the Buddhists of all lands.

"The possessor of the Tooth of Buddha will have the dominion of the World." Thus runs the ancient fiat, and a thoughtful French admiral told his compatriots the other day that this proud position had actually been attained by Britain. But he did not, of course, attribute it to the possession of the Tooth of Buddha, or indeed mention that object at all. He showed that the British fleet possessed an astounding power, which he strongly advised his compatriots not to undervalue.

But there is moral force as well as physical power; and the position of Her Gracious Majesty in the world is certainly unique. She holds in her dominions the most vital sections of all the great religions of the past. Her subjects pray to Christ, and Buddha, and Brahma, and Jehovah. They honour Zarathustra, and Moses, and Mahomet. Benares, the holy city of the greatest religious section of her subjects, is in her domains. The most intelligent of the Mussulman populations flourish peaceably in Delhi and the other Indian cities, where their creed of old attained its greatest triumphs. The Buddhists of Burmah and Ceylon are more enlightened than the Buddhists of other lands. No wonder that thoughtful minds begin to see in all this a possible mission for England, namely, to fuse the creeds of the world in one great crucible and eliminate the superstitious parts. Ancient creeds had much in common, and it is this common portion, the vital essence, that has been allowed to evaporate.

A short time ago a writer in the *Revue des Deux Mondes* announced that the Nineteenth Century had experienced two great surprises. The first was the discovery, due to Colebrooke and the earlier Sanskrit scholars, that the poems of early Greece were not altogether original. Jove and his Mount Olympus had been anticipated by Indra and his Mount Meru; the feats of Hercules had been matched by Bhîma. Parnassus and Apollo and the Muses had prototypes in Mount Govudun, redolent with the music of Kṛishna and the Gopîs; and that even the great hordes of gods and men, and their muster to avenge the rape of a pretty woman, had been previously made into a great epic on the banks of the Ganges.

The seeond surprise was perhaps more important. It was discovered that the loftier ideals of Christianity, its substitution of the principle of forgiveness for that of revenge, its broad catholicity, its missionary energy, and even its rites and parabolic legends, were due to an earlier religious reformer. Of him this little work proposes to treat. If these last statements can be substantiated, Buddha without doubt may take his place amongst the "Epoch-Makers of the World."

There are converts and converts. If a man is forced to kneel down, if his neck is laid bare and another man with a scimitar then and there induces him to accept certain creed-formulas, his case in one sense may be called a conversion. The same may be said of a man in a combustible dress tied to a stake and threatened with burning faggots and a lighted torch. But Buddhist conversions differ in this, that the man with the bare neck converts the man with the sword, the man with the combustible dress converts the man with the torch. Islam in its early strength advanced to root out Buddhism in Persia, Egypt, Asia Minor. The result was that half the conquering phalanx became Buddhists. The Crusaders strove to root out Islam, with a similar result. The Society of the Rose made a conquest of the Templars and other Knights Hospitallers, and these brought back to Europe Buddhism and the Reformation.

The first modern study of Buddhism commenced in one of our colonies. It was conducted chiefly by the missionaries for missionary purposes; and great credit is due to the missionaries of Ceylon for their scholarship, their industry, their honesty. But once more the curious phenomenon began to be noticeable. The learned works written to "expose" Buddhism made no converts amongst the Buddhists, but many in Christendom. Schopenhauer led the way, and drew half the intelligence of Germany in his wake. Then came the startling works of Bishop Bigandet and the Abbé Huc. M. Léon de Rosny announced a short time ago that there were 20,000 Buddhists in Paris alone.

If the dead bones of an ancient creed can thus stir in the valley, it seems certainly worth while to inquire what that creed was like in the days of its youth and strength.

CONTENTS

BUDDHA AND BUDDHISM

CHAPTER I

INTRODUCTORY

Let us suppose that a "Day of Brahma," of the pattern imaged by Hindus, has, with mighty flames and vast streams of volcanic lava, burnt up the present race of mankind, and that by and by, in further fulfilment of Eastern dreams, a new race has developed. Let us suppose also that some individuals of this new race have discovered in a cave in Brittany two tractates miraculously preserved—the one a sort of ancestor-worship by a religious reformer named Comte, and the other by one "Catholicus," setting forth another scheme of ancestor or saint-worship, with pilgrimages to their shrines and temples, cures performed at holy tanks, remissions of future fire torture by the intercession of priests.

This discovery would, of course, make much noise in learned colleges, and in process of time the tractates would be deciphered, and it would be seen that one of these religions had plainly been derived from the other. Which was the earlier? This was warmly debated, until by and by the question, let us imagine, was settled to the satisfaction of all by a learned writer named Excelsior.

Excelsior showed that this man Comte (if he was a real man, and not a tendency) was a man of genius, a philosopher, a man of science. His main postulate was that religion, like everything else, must be based on the facts of experience, not the dreams of the imagination. His motto apparently was: "Man we know; God we do not know. Let us confine our cultus to the known. Let us honour the illustrious that have gone before us. Their exertions have made us what we are. We, too, may improve the race by our exertions here, and by our memory hereafter."

There was nothing really superstitious in the cultus of the man Comte, because it was admitted that the saints of this religion were really dead. They had passed into the great "Temple of Nothingness."

Excelsior then, in a few vigorous paragraphs, poured out his scorn on those who could imagine a man like Comte plagiarising the miserable superstitions of the creed of "Catholicus." It is plain that the latter was the scheme of Comte turned inside out, vulgarised, debased—probably by priests, for greed and power many centuries after the death of Comte.

In our learned colleges a similar topsy-turvy question has arisen. There are two Buddhisms. The first, on the surface, seems to have emerged from the rude saint deifications of the previous Brahminism. The temple in those days was the sepulchral mound, even when calcined ashes had replaced the corpse. The man Buddha was worshipped in such a temple. He was invoked in the Buddhist litany to appear at the altar during the sacrifice. He was asked to forgive sins. He was addressed by the titles that the Hindoos use towards their Supreme God. In the *White Lotus of Dharma* he is made to announce that a Buddha is an incarnation of Swayambhu, and that at death he goes back to rule the universe from his throne in the sky.

The second Buddhism, however, proclaimed that a dead Buddha was non-existent, and that Swayambhu himself was non-existent; but its cultus was the same as the other Buddhism. Its followers had the sepulchral *dâgoba*, or relic tumulus, as a temple, but devoid of relics. They asked Buddha to appear at the altar during worship. They asked him to forgive sins. They addressed him by the titles that the Hindoos use towards their Supreme God. Does not all this seem on the surface to have been the outcome of an innovating school, an atheistical school, altering dogma but unable to alter ritual? But the "Excelsiors" of our learned colleges will not admit of such an explanation, and it must be confessed that this topsy-turvy Buddhism has a real support in topsy-turvy Buddhist literature. The books, which some five hundred years after Buddha's death (under the collective title of the "Great Vehicle") revealed the Non-God seated on his throne of Nothingness, have also puzzling Sûtras announcing Eternal Life for all men in a paradise of an eternal God. This has allowed English writers on Buddhism to contend that the second school was the Deistical school—a privilege, however, that has been now completely taken away from them by the publication by Professor Max Müller of the Mahâyâna Sûtras in his collection, the *Sacred Books of the East*.

It is not too much to say that this publication has rendered obsolete the greater part of our English disquisitions on Buddhism. It shows:

1. That the innovating Buddhism of the "Great Vehicle" proclaimed the following:—

There is no God and no material world. Man comes from the Great Nothing, and after a brief dream of non-existing worlds returns to it. All this had already been given to the public by Brian Hodgson and Rajendra Lala Mitra, and also in my *Popular Life of Buddha.* I showed also from Hwen Thsang, the Chinese traveller, that this innovating Buddhism was forced upon the earlier Buddhism by King Kaniśka about A.D. 16.

2. But a new fact of crucial importance has emerged from this volume of the *Sacred Books of the East.* There was recoil as well as revolution. Bound up together in the same library are two philosophies and two religions—distinct, antagonistic, internecine. The eternal Buddha, Amitâyas, is a protest against the non-existent Buddha.

Brian Hodgson called the innovating atheism "Pyrrhonism," and by the aid of this *Mahâyâna Sûtras* in the *Sacred Books of the East* we can have no doubt as to what the Pyrrho-Buddha was like. From one of these *Sûtras,* entitled the "Diamond Cutter," I will give a little sketch of him.

But at starting I must point out that Pyrrhonism is scarcely the correct word for this school of Buddhism. Pyrrhonism doubted everything. Pyrrho-Buddhism had no doubts at all. The difference can be made clear if we suppose that Pyrrho and Śâkya Muni were both asked this question: "Have you seen the disciple

Subhûti this morning, and was his head bald, and did he wear the yellow cloak?"

The answer of Pyrrho would be after this fashion: "I have no sufficient evidence that I exist, nor can I get it. Such being the case, it must, of course, be doubtful to me whether I possess two eyes. And if I do not exist, doubts must also be thrown over the existence of the disciple Subhûti, his bald head, and his yellow cloak!"

The answer of the Pyrrho-Buddha would differ from this.

"It is an absolute certainty that I do not exist, and it is an absolute certainty that my two eyes do not exist. It is another absolute certainty that the disciple Subhûti does not exist, and a non-existent disciple must have a non-existent bald head, and a cloak equally intangible; but stop and listen to the whole of my revelation. Although it is an absolute certainty that the disciple Subhûti does not exist, it is also an absolute certainty that he does exist. It is a certainty equally absolute that his bald head exists, that his yellow cloak exists. It is an absolute certainty also that I, Buddha, do not exist, but it is also an absolute certainty that I do exist."

Now this Buddhism, which we may call the "Glad Tidings of Stupid Contradiction," runs through the whole of the Sûtra called the "Diamond Cutter." It is supposed to record a conversation between Buddha and the disciple Subhûti, in the Jetavana grove near Srâvastî. Buddha declares that in the course of his many transmigrations a Buddha delivers immeasurable millions of beings, and yet not one is ever delivered (p. 114). He declares that the coming Buddhas (Bodhisatwas) must have the most distinct conception of *Dharma* (spiritual religion), and also no conception of *Dharma* at all. They must have understanding, and no understanding (p. 117). He states that the Buddhas have preached the highest perfect knowledge, and that they have never preached the highest knowledge at all (p. 118). It affirms, too, that the Bodhisatwas who study the "Diamond Cutter" will be endowed with miraculous powers, and "frame to themselves a true idea. And why?—because a true idea is not a true idea! Therefore Buddha preaches 'A true idea, a true idea indeed'" (p. 126). It is said that the treatise is to be entitled the *Prajñâ Pâramitâ* (the Wisdom of the other Bank), because it is not the Wisdom of the other Bank. Therefore it is entitled *Prajñâ Pâramitâ* (p. 125).

Here is a specimen of the argument:

"Therefore, O Subhûti, a noble-minded *Bodhisatwa*, after putting aside all ideas, should raise his mind to the highest perfect knowledge. He should frame his mind so as not to believe in form, sound, smell, taste, or anything that can be touched. And why? Because what is believed is not believed. Therefore the Tathâgata preaches: A gift should not be given by a *Bodhisatwa* who believes in anything. It should not be given by one who believes in form, sound, smell, taste, or anything that can be touched."

Now all this could not be the work of an absolute lunatic. He must have had some motive for these apparently aimless contradictions. What was that motive? After exhausting all possible theories, I have come to this conclusion. The Pyrrho-Buddhists were confronted with the puzzling question of the earlier literature. They could not destroy it. It was determined to neutralise it by flooding it with contradictory passages; and to give a colour to this, a few Sûtras like the "Diamond Cutter" and the *Brahmajâla Sûtra* had to be composed to mystify people. Sir Monier Monier-Williams and Professor Rhys Davids prove Buddha to have been an athiest from the latter Sûtra. Its importance shall be dealt with further on.

But I must emphasise one point. Now that the Mahâyâna Sûtras can be examined by all, if any new writer still insists on depicting Pyrrho-Buddha as the real historical Buddha, he must give us the complete Pyrrho-Buddha,—the whole statue, not an arm or a nose. I will explain my meaning. Says Dr. Crozier in the *Fortnightly Review* for February:

"He (Buddha) threw out the Supreme Soul altogether as a piece of supererogation, finding that he could get on quite as well without it in his explanation of the world."

Now, if we take the "Diamond Cutter" or the *Brahmajâla Sûtra*, as representing accurately the talk by which Buddha democratised the chief religions of Asia and Europe, Dr. Crozier could no doubt prove his point; for if there is no God in existence, and no man at all, it is certain that no man can be a theist. But this is scarcely stating the whole case. It would be just as easy to write down a few other passages like the following:

"He (Buddha) threw out altogether the visible Kosmos as a piece of supererogation, finding that he could get on quite as well without it in his explanation of the Divine scheme."

Or this:

"He (Buddha) threw out altogether himself and his disciples as non-existent things, finding that he could get on very well without them in his grand project of giving *Dharma* to the world."

In my next chapter I will sketch religion in India at the date of Buddha's advent. This may help us to judge whether a Buddha or a Pyrrho-Buddha would be most likely to emerge. Evolution, not capricious originality, is the law of religious development.

CHAPTER II

THE RELIGION OF THE ṚISHI

In the earliest Indian epics, like the *Mahâbhârata*, we find no mention of temples, but a great deal about *Tîrthas*, or sacred tanks. "It is the greatest mystery of the Ṛishis, excellent son of Bharata. The holy pilgrimage to the Tîrthas is more important than sacrifices to the gods."[1]

In another verse it is stated that five nights' sojourn at the Tîrtha of Jambumârya is equal to the fruit of a horse sacrifice. The horse sacrifice was the most important of Âryan rites. A hundred performances of it raised the sacrificer to the level of Indra, the Supreme.

"May the pilgrim bathe, O son of Bharata, in all the Tîrthas."

Illustrious saints resided in Tîrthas, the dead as well as the living. Kapila has his Tîrtha, the Ṛishi Matanga, the Saint Bhrigu.

"Go where the greatest Ṛishis Valmîki and Kasyapa, Kundajathara, the son of Atri, Viśvâmitra, and Gautama, Asita Devala, Mârkandeya and Gâlava, Bharadwâja and the Solitary Vaśishṭha, Uddâlaka, Saunaka, and his son Vyâsa, the greatest of ascetics, Durvâsas, the most virtuous of anchorites, Jâvâli, of the terrible macerations; go where these, the

[1] Vana Parva, v. 4059.

greatest of saints, rich in penances, are waiting for thee."

What does all this mean?

Simply that the magical powers of a dead *Ṛishi*, or saint, were deemed much more potent than the magical powers of that saint when living. And that near his *stûpa*, or sepulchral mound, or near the modest tree where he was buried, a tank had been dug to take advantage of those powers. It gave drinking water to the worshippers, and could also magically cure diseases, like the tank of St. Anne at Auray in Brittany, and exercise other charms.

"When King Suhotra governed this globe according to the laws of justice, columns of sacrifice and sacred trees were planted about the surface of the earth [jalonnaient la terre—Fauçhe] in hundreds of thousands. They shone every season with an abundant harvest of men and grains."[1]

"He offered then, O most virtuous son of Bharata, an hundred solemn sacrifices, bidding gods and Brahmins. There were columns of sacrifice in precious stones and chaityas [sepulchral mounds] of gold."

"The Long-Haired God gave by thousands and millions columns of sacrifice aud chaityas of great splendour."

These allude to the dolmens and stone circles like our Abury and Macshow. They are spread all over India, and Dr. Stevenson, in the *Asiatic Journal*, points out that they are still being used. The holy tree was an earlier memorial of the saint, hero, medicine man; and it is very conspicuous at the holy places of pilgrimage, for it figures in the descriptions of the

[1] Mahâbhârata, Adi Parva, v. 3717.

Tîrthas that Yudhishthira in the Mahâbhârata was enjoined to visit.

"Where, as Brahmins tell, was born that Indian fig-tree of which the cause is eternal?" This was at Gayâ.[1]

At Yamounâ, too, it is announced: "There is the beautiful and the holy Tîrtha, named the Descent of the Holy Fig-Tree."

And when the heroes of the epic—Kṛishṇa, Bhîma, and Dhananjaya—assault an enemy's city, they at once run and demolish the sacred tree to ward off, most probably, hostile spells:

"Then they [Kṛishṇa, Bhîma, and Dhananjaya] rushed upon the splendid *chaitya* of the inhabitants of Magadha, and smote it on the crest as they wished to smite Jarâsandha.

"And with the blows of their great arms they felled that ancient tree, vast, firmly rooted, with airy top, respected by all, and ever honoured with incense and garlands."[2]

It is to be observed that for the rude earthen dome of the *stûpa*, for the more modern metal canopy or Baldechino, and for the sacred tree, the same Sanskrit word is applied, *chaitya* (the Kosmical Umbrella).

All this rather reminds us of the days of Clovis and his relic superstitions.

"How can we hope for victory if we offend St. Martin!"

This was his speech when he cut off the head of a soldier who had foraged a little hay in regions defended by the bones of St. Martin of Tours. And in his Spanish campaign the relics of St. Vincent at Saragossa

[1] Vana Parva. v. 8307. [2] Sabha Parva, v. 816.

proved more potent than many archers and mailed warriors, for the good king turned aside his army and fled away from them. Snorri Storlusen records that Woden gave orders that *haugs* (the counterpart of the Buddhist tope) should be erected over the calcined remains of heroes, and *batausten* (standing stones) over their bravest soldiers. But the tomb of the dead man was his dwelling-house in life. In India, from the date of the hymns of the Ṛig-Veda, the Srâddha or worship of the dead man, has been conspicuous. Here is a portion of one of them:

"We have amidst our ancestors, the Angirases, the Navagwas, the Atharvans, the Somyas; may we obtain their favour, their benign protection! O dead man [the corpse], come to us! Come by the ancient roads that our fathers have traversed before thee. Behold these two kings, Yama and the divine Varuṇa, who rejoice in our oblations.

"Come with the ancestors. Come with Yama to this altar which our piety has dressed. Thou hast cast off all impurity. Come to this domain and don a body of brilliance.

"O ancestors, disperse! Go every one to his own side. A place has been set apart for the departed one. Yama permits him to come down and enjoy our libations morning and night.

"Give our libation to Yama with Agni as a messenger. Offer to Yama a holocaust sweet as honey.

"Honour to the First Ones, the ancient Ṛishis who have shown us the way."

This ancestor-worship is still prevalent in India, and the dead man much propitiated. An English magistrate of hasty temper died some time ago. He was much feared by the natives, and to calm his spirit they kept it constantly supplied with glasses of strong brandy-and-water and very large cheroots.

But in process of time the burning of the corpse succeeded burial, and a quaint compromise occurred. Colebrooke tells us that even in modern times the calcined remains of a Hindoo are put into a pot and buried in a deep hole, and over the spot of the cremation a mound of masonry is formed, and a tree or a tank or a flag erected. The rich can afford a *Chettrî* of splendid marble. By and by this pot is dug up, and it and the ashes are thrown into the holy river. Here we have the tank-worship, the *stûpa*-worship, the tree-worship proving too strong for the cremating reformers. Perhaps, too, the Brahmins were loth to give up so lucrative a superstition.

My friend Major Keith, an officer who held a high post in the Archæological Department in India, tells me that at Lashkar, a spot rarely visited by white faces, he saw the statues of the three last Scindiahs, each under his Chettrî. Daily food and drink was served to these. Then rich *hookahs* were filled with exquisite tobacco, and beautiful dancing-girls jingled their bangles in front of the marble *Râjahs*.

Why places of pilgrimage in India were first called "Tanks," or *Tîrthas*, and why the name has stuck to the group of pilgrimage accessories—holy tree, relic *dâgopa*, *stûpa*, etc., we cannot tell, but we may make a plausible guess. First, the savage medicine man, much feared in life, was buried under a tree. Drinking water would be required for the crowd who came to his grave to gain spells and charms. Hence a pond would be dug. Then it would be found convenient to announce that this water was the main apparatus of the magic. Drink it or bathe in it and you could put an end at once to your neuralgic pains or your favourite enemy. No wonder that from an early date the Tîrtha was the chief word used for the shrines.

Then the dead man's cairn grew and grew, and when the remains were burnt a dâgopa was required for the calcined ashes. And soon utilitarian additions crept in.

In point of fact, astronomers and anthropologists in recent years have let us know the uses that the sepulchral dolmen or *stûpa* was put to. It was at once an observatory, a church clock, an almanac, a farmer's calendar, in days when church clocks and almanacs were not invented. And the shapeless, huge, imposing stone gods that surrounded it were part of the apparatus of the astronomer. One of the earliest constructed dwellings of the savage man in a cold climate was probably a tiny chamber of boughs and loose stones, with a covering of earth for warmth. Such dwellings are numerous in Lapland, and in the Orkneys and many parts of Scotland their ruins figure under the title of "Picts' Houses." From the cairn came the tope.

We now come to an important point, the religions that the man on the top of the *stûpa* evolved from watching stars and sunsets and sunrises.

Says Colebrooke of the Ṛig-Veda: "The deities invoked appear, on a cursory inspection of the Veda, to be as various as the authors of the prayers addressed to them; but, according to the most ancient annotations of the Indian scripture, these numerous names of persons and things are all resolvable into different titles of three deities, and ultimately of one God."[1]

[1] Colebrooke, *Essays*, vol. i. p. 25.

Wilson, the Orientalist, follows suit and tells us that it is specially announced by an old Indian commentator of the Vedas that the various names, Mitra, Agni, Pushan, Bhaga, etc., are merely applied to the sun in reference to his various halting-places during his yearly journey.[1]

The twelve gods were also called the Twelve Âdityas, or Months. Aditî, the mighty Mother, had twelve sons. She and Varuṇa and Mitra—matter, Spirit, and the Sun—were probably the Trinity in Unity to which Colebrooke alludes.

"They [the Brahmins] have always observed the order of the gods as they are to be worshipped in the twelvemonth," says the Ṛig-Veda (vii. 103).

"The year is Prajâpati [the Divine Man]," says the Aitareya Brahmaṇa.

"Thou dividest thy person in twelve parts," says a hymn of the Mahâbhârata to the divinity, "and thou becomest the Twelve Âdityas."[2]

The "God in twelve persons" is another expression from the same poem.

"These pillars, ranging in rows like swans, have come to us erected by pious Ṛishis to the East. They proceed resplendent on the path of the gods."

The Sanskrit word for an upright unhewn monolith is "stambha." The same word was used later on for the temporary "posts" erected during a horse sacrifice. A monolith is also called "Mahâdeo" (Great God), even in modern times.

Much unwisdom has been written about the hymns of the Ṛig-Veda, owing to the fact that the writers

[1] Wilson's note, *Rig-Veda*, vol. i. p. 34.

[2] Vana Parva, v. 189.

ignored the close connection between the standing stones and the hymns. In point of fact, at an early date the Ṛishi on the top of the *stûpa* judged that if man was to have any outside religious rites at all, he should seek to combine harmoniously his knowledge and his lofty dreams. His rites should be at once utilitarian and theological. He judged that as the year marched along the ecliptic from stone god to stone god, the worship of each should illustrate the changes. The Vedic zodiac, and the rites and symbolism attached to it, I have fully treated in my *Buddhism in Christendom*, chap. xxiii.

Colebrooke gives us the early Nakshetras (lunar mansions), and we find each called after Aditî, Varuṇa, or some other Vedic god. But the man on the *stûpa* soon observed that most of these gods disappeared after a time, but that the pole star and the Great Bear never disappeared. They became, the first, the throne of the Almighty, and the second, the Seven Ṛishis. From the extravagant way in which the Seven Great Sages are talked of in the sacred books, one might imagine at times that the Hindoos believe in a sort of Committee-God, seven dead men ruling the universe by concerted acts. But the *stûpa* had become a place of pilgrimage. Its tank could cure aches and pains. And the Karma of the dead saint could bring good fortune to the pilgrim in the next world, or, better still, in this.

"The holy pilgrimage to the Tîrthas," says the Mahâbhârata, "is more important than the sacrifice to the Gods."

Plainly the Brahmins soon saw this, and see it still. Indian Râjahs to this day are mulcted of enormous sums when they go to the shrine of some dead saint to cure a beloved daughter or straighten a crooked leg.

But if these Seven Great Ṛishis were taken over by the earliest Buddhists and worshipped as the Seven Great Manushi Buddhas; if, moreover, the outside religion of early Buddhism consisted almost entirely in erecting *stûpas* in their honour and feeding them daily with food, it is difficult to believe that the early Buddhists would have done such things if they held that these Buddhas were non-existent, and the spiritual world a delusion.

The religions of the world are indebted to the Ṛishi and his *stûpa* for other noticeable ideas.

Says a clever Indian thinker: "No lower conception than that of an Absolute and Infinite Divinity could satisfy indomitable Reason. Yet how could such a Being be brought into relation with matter; and if perfect goodness is one of his Attributes, whence then came sin into the world? Into this labyrinth of insoluble, obstinate questionings the professors of the Divine Science plunged deep. They detached the act of creation from the Absolute Being, whom they could not conceive as Unconditioned, yet acting upon matter. They expanded the notion of the Divine Idea hypostatised. They invented the Demi-urge, or secondary Creative Agent. They bridged over the gulf between the Intelligible and the Phenomenal by various logical formulas, and a series of graduated abstractions. They personified the divine attributes."[1]

This is true, and again the man on the *stûpa*, fond of

[1] The "Theological Situation in India," in the *Fortnightly* for November 1898, by Vamadeo Shastri.

2

symbols, seems to have been at work. It appeared to him as it did to every one else in ancient days, that the universe was a large umbrella, with the mighty earth for a basis and the pole star for a pivot round which the umbrella whirled. The interior of this umbrella was lit up by stars fastened to it, but outside was a dark mysterious Ocean, where the light never penetrated. Within this was placed the Uncònditioned, and the man on the *stûpa* invented a Vice-god.

I will condense a hymn of the Ṛig-Veda:

> "There was no breath, no sky, but water only—
> Death was not yet unwombed, nor day nor night.
> The unimagined THAT ONE, veiled and lonely,
> Sate through the centuries devoid of light.
>
> Then from his impulse Love came into being,
> And through the ebon blackness flung his beams,
> That Love which, say our men of mystic seeing,
> Bridges the world of fact and world of dreams.
>
> . . . .
>
> O tell us how this universe was fashioned,
> Ere shining gods appeared to men below?—
> He knows—the shrouded THAT ONE unimpassioned!
> Or even he perchance can never know."

THAT ONE is *Tad* in Sanskrit; Love is *Kâma.*

These two portions of the heavens in Buddhism, as in Brahmanism, are called *Nirvṛitti* and *Pravṛitti.* *Nirvṛitti* is derived from two words—*Nir,* the Sanskrit privative, and *vṛitti,* action (from the root-word *vṛit,* to move). *Nirvṛitti* is thus the quiescent portion of the sky inhabited by Brahma. And Brian Hodgson, when conversing with the intelligent Buddhist, Amirta Nanda Bandhya in Nepal, was astonished to find that the bugaboo word Nirvâṇa, the terror of many

Christian treatises, simply expressed the same idea: Nir—privative, *vâṇa*—breath.

"As a man fond of gay clothing, throwing off a corpse bound to his shoulders, goes away rejoicing, so must I, throwing off this perishable body and freed from all desires, enter the City of Nirvâṇa (Nirvâṇa-pura)."[1]

And when the gods come to salute this infant Buddha in the temple, these words were a part of their hymn:

> "Like the sun, the sea and Meru mount
> Is Swayambhu, the self-existent God,
> And all who do him homage shall obtain
> Heaven and Nirvṛitti."[2]

In the earliest Buddhism, *Nirvṛitti* was the abode of Brahma. This is what the Buddhas of the Past say to the young Buddha when they urge him to forsake the lower for the higher life:

"Stablish thy flock in the way of Brahma and of the ten virtues, that when they pass away from among their fellow-men they may all go to the abode of Brahma."[3]

In point of fact, Buddha called his followers Brahmins, and was a Brahmin himself, though a reforming one. And the *Satapatha Brâhmaṇa* and other Indian books used the word Buddha, it must be mentioned, for the yogi who in the silences of the forest had attained the great spiritual awakening.[4] The word *Brahma Nirvâṇa*, or blissful union with Brahma, occurs several times in the Mahâbhârata; and Colebrooke and Goldstucker tell us that in the earliest days it did not mean annihilation at all.

[1] *Birth Stories*, p. 6. [2] *Lalita Vistara.* [3] *Ibid.*

[4] *Satapatha Brâhmaṇa*, xiv. 7. 2. 17. See also Manu, iv. 204.

Now, oddly enough, this ambition of the poor Indian Ṛishi to solve the mighty mystery of the Unconditioned is the very feature in his philosophy that Sir Monier Monier-Williams is most angry with him about.

"It is obvious that to believe in the ultimate merging of man's personal spirit in One Impersonal Spirit is virtually to deny the ultimate existence of any human spirit at all. Nay more, it is virtually to deny the existence of a supreme universal spirit also. For how can a merely abstract universal spirit, which is unconscious of personality, be regarded as possessing any real existence worth being called true life."[1]

But is not this rather dangerous ground for an author whose lectures are, almost avowedly, less an exposition of an Indian religion than discourses on a Scotch form of Christianity. St. John tells us that the world was made by Christ (i. 10), and also that "the Father judgeth no man, but hath committed all judgment to the Son" (v. 22). We learn also from Hebrews (i. 3) that Christ "upholds" the Kosmos. Surely here we have the active Logos and the inactive (Tertullian calls him the "invisible, unapproachable, placid") "Father." St. Augustine based his entire Christianity on the text (John xiv. 23): "Jesus answered and said unto him, If a man love Me, he will keep My words: and My Father will love him, and We will come unto him, and make Our abode with him." And there is scarcely a doubt now with scholars that the early Christians borrowed the solution of earth's mighty problem from India. Christianity—at least the Alexandrian portion of it—

[1] *Buddhism*, p. 106.

is gnosticism, and gnosticism is the word *Bodhi* transferred to the Greek. *Buthos*, the abode of the inactive Father, is *Nirvṛitti*; and the illuminated *Pleroma*, presided over by Christ, is the *Pravṛitti* of the Buddhists.

It was the Father's good pleasure that in Him the whole Pleroma should have its home (Col. i. 19). In Him dwells the whole Pleroma of the Godhead in bodily shape (Col. ii. 9).[1]

To sum up, I think in this chapter I have shown—

1. That the religious cultus of India at the date of Buddha's birth was a sort of saint-worship and ghost-worship.

2. That the first rude temple had emerged from the sepulchral mound of the saint. This mound had become an observatory, which taught the proper seasons of sowing and tilling. It furnished great tanks when water was scarce. It was a beehive dome from whence flew many religions and philosophies.

3. That the stars, as viewed from this dome, were the early gods of the earth. Indeed, the Hindoo lunar mansions were called Aditî, Varuṇa, etc.

4. That great prominence was given to the seven stars of the Great Bear. All other stars seemed to sink into the earth. Hence the legend of the death of the gods. But the seven stars of the Bear were viewed as the immortal homes of seven legions of spirits, each provided over by a Ṛishi, or saint.

[1] All that is written in this work combating the views of Sir Monier Monier-Williams was finished whilst he was still alive. If the dogmatisms of the day prevented him from properly sympathising with Indian thought, it is to be admitted that his work as a great Sanskrit scholar has been most valuable.

5. That trees also were worshipped "with incense and garlands,"—an earlier form perhaps of saint-worship, when the saint's grave was under a tree in a forest. The seven mortal Buddhas had each his tree.

6. That as early as the hymns of the Ṛig-Veda we see the idea of an inactive god with a vice-god, a logos, a dead mortal, to do his work. Yama and Manu figure thus. The latter in one hymn is announced as the creator of the sun. This meets, I think, General Maisey's contention that Buddhism was derived from the Jews. The latter have always hated the triad conception. I think also that it affects what we may call Pyrrho-Buddha theories. A man in rags going about and proclaiming, "You come from nothing, my brethren;—you are going back to nothing. Brahma is nothing; Râma is nothing; Manu, the non-existent, never created a non-existent sun. Nirvṛitti is nothing, and nowhere; Pravṛitti is nothing, and nowhere; the Seven Ṛishis are nothing, and nowhere. Your sacred tanks have no healing powers. The saint's bones under the *stûpa* can do no good to your rheumatism, for they, you, it, and I, are all non-existent." Such a Buddha would certainly have less chance of being listened to than a Buddha whose change was a gentle evolution rather than a root-and-branch demolition and rebuilding,—one, in fact, who retained the higher elements of the previous religion and only modified the lower.

For in hymns of the Ṛig-Veda, said by Max Müller to have been composed at least three thousand years ago, we learn that the Ṛishi Ṛibhu retired to a forest to perform penance and gain wisdom.[1] Yama, too,

[1] Ṛig-Veda, i. 7, 24.

the Indian Adam, we are told, "conversed with gods under a leafy tree." Century after century has rolled away, yet still the Indian yogi, clad in his poor bark, squats on his deerskin, and calmly watches the panorama of history pass on before him. He has seen the early cattle-lifters and bowmen of the Five Rivers. He has seen Alexander clad in shining mail, and Nadir Shah smeared all over with diamonds and blood. He has seen the great noses and great cocked hats of great Wellington and great Napier. He has seen Aśoka the tolerant, Râma the loving, and the great Tathâgata, Buddha himself. Gods and creeds and philosophies he has imagined in his mystic reverie, and scattered them broadcast amongst the nations of the earth. Calmly he squats on the antelope's skin, like John in his raiment of camel's hair.

CHAPTER III

BUDDHA

BUDDHA was born at Kapilavastu, in the Lumbini Garden, B.C. 550.

Kapilavastu—the City of Kapila. This is the translation of the word. Much has been made by some Orientalists of this. The City of Kapila, the author of the Niriswara, or Atheistic Sankhya philosophy, is evidently, it has been urged, a non-existent place, and Buddha a non-existent person. He is a myth invented to shadow forth the dissemination of Kapila's atheism. But nothing is certain except the unexpected. The non-existing city has suddenly turned up, covering miles of jungle.

Sir Alexander Cunningham, the great Indian archæologist, was of opinion that the site of Kapilavastu was Bhuila, in the Basti district. But the real site is now no matter of doubt. It is between Gorukhpore and the Himalayas.

In 1893 a pillar was discovered in the Nepal Terai, the mighty forest that surrounds the great Himalayan range. Deciphered, it proved to be one of the columns of King Aśoka, who covered India with his stone inscriptions, B.C. 257. It announced that on this particular spot was the *stúpa* of Kanaka Muni, one of the seven great mortal Buddhas. In the year 1896

Major Waddell pointed out, in the *Journal of the Asiatic Society of Bengal*, that, according to the testimony of Hwen Thsang, the celebrated Chinese traveller, this *stûpa* was only seven miles off from Buddha's birthplace, the traveller having paid it a visit. This brought Dr. Führer into the field, and he was soon rewarded with the discovery of an inscription identifying the celebrated Lumbini Garden where Queen Mâyâ gave birth to her distinguished son. Then came a second triumph. Choked up in the luxurious jungle by colossal ferns and creepers emerged a dead city of *stûpas*, and monasteries, and villages and buildings. More important still was another column set up by King Aśoka. This is the translation of it:

"King Piyadasi (Aśoka), the beloved of the gods, having been anointed twenty years, himself came and worshipped, saying, 'Here Buddha, Śâkya Muni, was born!' And he caused a stone pillar to be erected, which declares, 'Here the Venerable was born.'"

I propose now to give a short life of Buddha. It has curious points of contact with that of Jesus.

Pre-Existence in Heaven

The early Buddhists, as we have seen, following the example of the Vedic Brahmins, divided space into Nirvṛitti, the dark portion of the heavens, and Pravṛitti, the starry systems. Over this last, the luminous portion, Buddha figures as ruler when the legendary life opens. The Christian Gnostics took over this idea and gave to Christ a similar function. He ruled the Pleroma.

"Behold a Virgin shall Conceive"

Exactly 550 years before Christ there dwelt in Kapilavastu a king called Śuddhodana. This monarch was informed by angels that a mighty teacher of men would be born miraculously in the womb of his wife. "By the consent of the king," says the *Lalita Vistara*, "the queen was permitted to lead the life of a virgin for thirty-two months." Joseph is made, a little awkwardly, to give a similar privilege to his wife (Matt. i. 25).

Some writers have called in question the statement that Buddha was born of a virgin, but in the southern scriptures, as given by Mr. Turnour, it is announced that a womb in which a Buddha elect has reposed is like the sanctuary of a temple. On that account, that her womb may be sacred, the mother of a Buddha always dies in seven days. The name of the queen was borrowed from Brahminism. She was Mâyâ Devî, the Queen of Heaven. And one of the titles of this lady is Kanyâ, the Virgin of the Zodiac.

Queen Mâyâ was chosen for her mighty privilege because the Buddhist scriptures announce that the mother of a Buddha must be of royal line.

Long genealogies, very like those of the New Testament, are given also to prove the blue blood of King Śuddhodana, who, like Joseph, had nothing to do with the paternity of the child. "King Mahasammata had a son named Roja, whose son was Vararoja, whose son was Kalyâna, whose son was Varakalyâna," and so on, and so on.[1]

How does a Buddha come down to earth? This

[1] Dîpawanso, see *Journ. As. Soc.*, Bengal, vol. vii. p. 925.

question is debated in Heaven, and the Vedas were searched because, as Seydel shows, although Buddhism seemed a root and branch change, it was attempted to show that it was really the lofty side of the old Brahminism, a lesson not lost by and by in Palestine. The sign of Capricorn in the old Indian Zodiac is an elephant issuing from a Makara (leviathan), and it symbolises the active god issuing from the quiescent god in his home on the face of the waters. In consequence, Buddha comes down as a white elephant, and enters the right side of the queen without piercing it or in any way injuring it. Childers sees a great analogy in all this to the Catholic theory of the perpetual virginity of Mary. Catholic doctors quote this passage from Ezekiel (xliv. 2):

"Then said the LORD unto me; This gate shall be shut, it shall not be opened, and no man shall enter by it; because the LORD, the God of Israel, hath entered in by it, therefore shall it be shut."

A Double Annunciation

It is recorded that when Queen Mâyâ received the supernal Buddha in her womb, in the form of a beautiful white elephant, she said to her husband: "Like snow and silver, outshining the sun and the moon, a white elephant of six tusks, with unrivalled trunk and feet, has entered my womb. Listen, I saw the three regions (earth, heaven, hell), with a great light shining in the darkness, and myriads of spirits sang my praises in the sky."

A similar miraculous communication was made to King Śuddhodana:

"The spirits of the Pure Abode flying in the air, showed half of their forms, and hymned King Śuddhodana thus—

> "Guerdoned with righteousness and gentle pity,
> Adored on earth and in the shining sky,
> The coming Buddha quits the glorious spheres
> And hies to earth to gentle Mâyâ's womb."

In the Christian scriptures there is also a double annunciation. In Luke (i. 28) the angel Gabriel is said to have appeared to the Virgin Mary before her conception, and to have foretold to her the miraculous birth of Christ. But in spite of this astounding miracle, Joseph seems to have required a second personal one before he ceased to question the chastity of his wife (Matt. i. 19). Plainly, two evangelists have been working the same mine independently, and a want of consistency is the result.

When Buddha was in his mother's womb that womb was transparent. The Virgin Mary was thus represented in mediæval frescoes.[1]

"We have seen his Star in the East"

In the Buddhist legend the devas in heaven announce that Buddha will be born when the Flower-star is seen *in the East.*[2]

Amongst the thirty-two signs that indicate the mother of a Buddha, the fifth is that, like Mary the mother of Jesus, she should be "on a journey"[3] at the moment of parturition. This happened. A tree

[1] See illustration, p. 39, in my *Buddhism in Christendom*

[2] Lefman, xxi. 124; Wassiljew, p. 95

[3] Beal, *Rom. History*, p. 32.

(palâsa, the scarlet butea) bent down its branches and overshadowed her, and Buddha came forth. Voltaire says that in the library of Berne there is a copy of the First Gospel of the Infancy, which records that a palm-tree bent down in a similar manner to Mary.[1] The Koran calls it a "withered date-tree."

In the First Gospel of the Infancy it is stated that, when Christ was in His cradle, He said to His mother: "I am Jesus, the Son of God, the Word whom thou didst bring forth according to the declaration of the angel Gabriel to thee, and my Father hath sent Me for the salvation of the world."

In the Buddhist scriptures it is announced that Buddha, on seeing the light said:

"I am in my last birth. None is my equal. I have come to conquer death, sickness, old age. I have come to subdue the spirit of evil, and give peace and joy to the souls tormented in hell."

In the same scriptures[2] it is announced that at the birth of the Divine child, the devas (angels) in the sky sang "their hymns and praises."

CHILD-NAMING

"Five days after the birth of Buddha," says Bishop Bigandet, in the *Burmese Life*, "was performed the ceremony of head ablution and naming the child" (p. 49).

We see from this where the ceremony of head ablution and naming the child comes from. In the *Lalita Vistara*, Buddha is carried to the temple. Plainly, we have the same ceremony. There the

[1] *Œuvres*, vol. xl.

[2] See Beal, *Rom. History*, p. 46.

idols bow down to him as in the First Gospel of the Infancy the idol in Egypt bows down to Jesus. In Luke the infant Jesus is also taken to the temple by his parents, to "do for him after the custom of the law (Luke ii. 27). What law? Certainly not the Jewish.

Herod and the Wise Men

It is recorded in the Chinese life[1] that King Bimbisâra, the monarch of Râjâgṛiha, was told by his ministers that a boy was alive for whom the stars predicted a mighty destiny. They advised him to raise an army and go and destroy this child, lest he should one day subvert the king's throne. Bimbisâra refused.

At the birth of Buddha the four Mahârâjas, the great Kings, who in Hindoo astronomy guard each a cardinal point, received him. These may throw light on the traditional Persian kings that greeted Christ.

In some quarters these analogies are admitted, but it is said that the Buddhists copied from the Christian scriptures. But this question is a little complicated by the fact that many of the most noticeable similarities are in apocryphal gospels, those that were abandoned by the Church at an early date. In the Protevangelion, at Christ's birth, certain marvels are visible. The clouds are "astonished," and the birds of the air stop in their flight. The dispersed sheep of some shepherds near cease to gambol, and the shepherds to beat them. The kids near a river are arrested with their mouths close to the water. All nature seems to pause for a mighty effort. In the

[1] Beal, *Rom. History*, p. 103.

Lalita Vistara the birds also pause in their flight when Buddha comes to the womb of Queen Mâyâ. Fires go out, and rivers are suddenly arrested in their flow.

More noticeable is the story of Asita, the Indian Simeon.

Asita dwells on Himavat, the holy mount of the Hindoos, as Simeon dwells on Mount Zion. The "Holy Ghost is upon" Simeon. That means that he has obtained the faculties of the prophet by mystical training. He "comes by the Spirit" into the temple. Asita is an ascetic, who has acquired the eight magical faculties, one of which is the faculty of visiting the Tawatinsa heavens. Happening to soar up into those pure regions one day, he is told by a host of devatas, or heavenly spirits, that a mighty Buddha is born in the world, "who will establish the supremacy of the Buddhist Dharma." The *Lalita Vistara* announces that, "looking abroad with his divine eye, and considering the kingdoms of India, he saw in the great city of Kapilavastu, in the palace of King Śuddhodana, the child shining with the glitter of pure deeds, and adored by all the worlds." Afar through the skies the spirits of heaven in crowds recited the "hymn of Buddha."

This is the description of Simeon in the First Gospel of the Infancy, ii. 6: "At that time old Simeon saw Him (Christ) shining as a pillar of light when St. Mary the Virgin, His mother, carried Him in her arms, and was filled with the greatest pleasure at the sight. And the angels stood around Him, adoring Him as a King; guards stood around Him."

Asita pays a visit to the king. Asita takes the little child in his arms. Asita weeps.

"Wherefore these tears, O holy man?"

"I weep because this child will be the great Buddha, and I shall not be alive to witness the fact."

The points of contact between Simeon and Asita are very close. Both are men of God, "full of the Holy Ghost." Both are brought "by the Spirit" into the presence of the Holy Child, for the express purpose of foretelling His destiny as the Anointed One.

More remarkable still is the incident of the disputation with the doctors.

A little Brahmin was "initiated," girt with the holy thread, etc., at eight, and put under the tuition of a holy man. When Viśvâmitra, Buddha's teacher, proposed to teach him the alphabet, the young prince went off:

"In sounding 'A,' pronounce it as in the sound of the word 'anitya.'

"In sounding 'I,' pronounce it as in the word 'indriya.'

"In sounding 'U,' pronounce it as in the word 'upagupta.'"

And so on through the whole Sanskrit alphabet.

In the first Gospel of the Infancy, chap. xx., it is recorded that when taken to the schoolmaster Zaccheus,

"The Lord Jesus explained to him the meaning of the letters Aleph and Beth.

"8. Also, which were the straight figures of the letters, which were the oblique, and what letters had double figures; which had points and which had none; why one letter went before another; and many other things He began to tell Him and explain, of which the master himself had never heard, nor read in any book.

"9. The Lord Jesus further said to the master, Take notice how I say to thee. Then He began clearly and distinctly to say Aleph, Beth, Gimel, Daleth, and so on to the end of the alphabet.

"10. At this the master was so surprised that he said, I believe this boy was born before Noah."

In the *Lalita Vistara* there are two separate accounts of Buddha showing his marvellous knowledge. His great display is when he competes for his wife. He then exhibits his familiarity with all lore, sacred and profane, "astronomy," the "syllogism," medicine, mystic rites.

The disputation with the doctors is considerably amplified in the 21st chapter of the First Gospel of the Infancy:

"5. Then a certain principal rabbi asked Him, Hast Thou read books?

"6. Jesus answered that He had read both books and the things which were contained in books.

"7. And he explained to them the books of the law and precepts and statutes, and the mysteries which are contained in the books of the prophets—things which the mind of no creature could reach.

"8. Then said that rabbi, I never yet have seen or heard of such knowledge! What do you think that boy will be?

"9. Then a certain astronomer who was present asked the Lord Jesus whether He had studied astronomy.

"10. The Lord Jesus replied, and told him the number of the spheres and heavenly bodies, as also their triangular, square, and sextile aspects, their progressive and retrograde motions, their size and several prognostications, and other things which the reason of man had never discovered.

"11. There was also among them a philosopher, well skilled in physic and natural philosophy, who asked the Lord Jesus whether He had studied physic.

"12. He replied, and explained to him physics and metaphysics.

"13. Also those things which were above and below the power of nature.

"14. The powers also of the body, its humours and their effects.

"15. Also the number of its bones, veins, arteries, and nerves.

"16. The several constitutions of body, hot and dry, cold and moist, and the tendencies of them.

"17. How the soul operated on the body.

"18. What its various sensations and faculties were.

"19. The faculty of speaking, anger, desire.

"20. And lastly, the manner of its composition and dissolution, and other things which the understanding of no creature had ever reached.

"21. Then that philosopher worshipped the Lord Jesus, and said, O Lord Jesus, from henceforth I will be Thy disciple and servant."

Viśvâmitra in like manner worshipped Buddha by falling at his feet.

The Four Presaging Tokens

Soothsayers were consulted by King Śuddhodana. They pronounced the following:—

"The young boy will, without doubt, be either a king of kings or a great Buddha. If he is destined to be a great Buddha, four presaging tokens will make his mission plain. He will see—

"1. An old man.

"2. A sick man.

"3. A corpse.

"4. A holy recluse.

"If he fails to see these four presaging tokens of an avatâra, he will be simply a Chakravartin" (king of earthly kings).

King Śuddhodana, who was a trifle worldly, was very much comforted by the last prediction of the soothsayers. He thought in his heart, It will be an easy thing to keep these four presaging tokens from the young prince. So he gave orders that three magnificent palaces should at once be built—the Palace of Spring, the Palace of Summer, the Palace of Winter. These palaces, as we learn from the *Lalita Vistara,* were the most beautiful palaces ever conceived on earth. Indeed, they were quite able to cope in splendour with Vaijayanta, the immortal palace of Indra himself. Costly pavilions were built out in all directions, with ornamented porticoes and burnished doors. Turrets and pinnacles soared into the sky. Dainty little windows gave light to the rich apartments. Galleries, balustrades, and delicate trellis-work were abundant everywhere. A thousand bells tinkled on each roof. We seem to have the lacquered

Chinese edifices of the pattern which architects believe to have flourished in early India. The gardens of these fine palaces rivalled the chess-board in the rectangular exactitude of their parterres and trellis-work bowers. Cool lakes nursed on their calm bosoms storks and cranes, wild geese and tame swans; ducks, also, as parti-coloured as the white, red, and blue lotuses amongst which they swam. Bending to these lakes were bowery trees—the champak, the acacia serisha, and the beautiful asoka tree with its orange-scarlet flowers. Above rustled the mimosa, the fan-palm, and the feathery pippala, Buddha's tree. The air was heavy with the strong scent of the tuberose and the Arabian jasmine.

It must be mentioned that strong ramparts were prepared round the palaces of Kapilavastu, to keep out all old men, sick men, and recluses, and, I must add, to keep in the prince.

And a more potent safeguard still was designed. When the prince was old enough to marry, his palace was deluged with beautiful women. He revelled in the "five dusts," as the Chinese version puts it. But a shock was preparing for King Śuddhodana.

This is how the matter came about. The king had prepared a garden even more beautiful than the garden of the Palace of Summer. A soothsayer had told him that if he could succeed in showing the prince this garden, the prince would be content to remain in it with his wives for ever. No task seemed easier than this, so it was arranged that on a certain day the prince should be driven thither in his chariot. But, of course, immense precautions had to be taken to keep all old men and sick men and corpses from his sight. Quite an army of soldiers were told off for this duty, and the city was decked with flags. The path of the prince was strewn with flowers and scents, and adorned with vases of the rich kadali plant. Above were costly hangings and garlands, and pagodas of bells.

But, lo and behold! as the prince was driving along, plump under the wheels of his chariot, and before the very noses of the silken nobles and the warriors with javelins and shields, he saw an unusual sight. This was an old man, very decrepit and very broken. The veins and nerves of his body were swollen and prominent; his teeth chattered; he was wrinkled, bald, and his few remaining hairs were of dazzling whiteness; he was bent very nearly double, and tottered feebly along, supported by a stick.

"What is this, O coachman?" said the prince. "A man with his blood all dried up, and his muscles glued to his body! His head is white; his teeth knock together; he is scarcely able to move along, even with the aid of that stick!"

"Prince," said the coachman, "this is Old Age. This man's senses are dulled; suffering has destroyed his spirit; he is contemned by his neighbours. Unable to help himself, he has been abandoned in this forest."

"Is this a peculiarity of his family?" demanded the prince, "or is it the law of the world? Tell me quickly."

"Prince," said the coachman, "it is neither a law of his family, nor a law of the kingdom. In every being youth is conquered by age. Your own father and mother and all your relations will end in old age. There is no other issue to humanity."

"Then youth is blind and ignorant," said the prince, "and sees not the future. If this body is to be the abode of old age, what have I to do with pleasure and its intoxications? Turn round the chariot, and drive me back to the palace!"

Consternation was in the minds of all the courtiers at this untoward occurrence; but the odd circumstance of all was that no one was ever able to bring to condign punishment the miserable author of the mischief. The old man could never be found.

King Śuddhodana was at first quite beside himself with tribulation. Soldiers were summoned from the distant provinces, and a cordon of detachments thrown out to a distance of four miles in each direction, to keep the other presaging tokens from the prince. By and by the king became a little more quieted. A ridiculous accident had interfered with his plans: "If my son could see the Garden of Happiness he never would become a hermit." The king determined that another attempt should be made. But this time the precautions were doubled.

On the first occasion the prince left the Palace of Summer by the eastern gate. The second expedition went through the southern gate.

But another untoward event occurred. As the prince was driving along in his chariot, suddenly he saw close to him a man emaciated, ill, loathsome, burning with fever. Companionless, uncared for, he tottered along, breathing with extreme difficulty.

"Coachman," said the prince, "what is this man, livid and loathsome in body, whose senses are dulled, and whose limbs are withered? His stomach is oppressing him; he is covered with filth. Scarcely can he draw the breath of life!"

"Prince," said the coachman, "this is Sickness. This poor man is attacked with a grievous malady. Strength and Comfort have shunned him. He is friendless, hopeless, without a country, without an asylum. The fear of death is before his eyes."

"If the health of man," said Buddha, "is but the sport of a dream, and the fear of coming evils can put on so loathsome a shape, how can the wise man, who has seen what life really means, indulge in its vain delights? Turn back, coachman, and drive me to the palace!"

The angry king, when he heard what had occurred, gave orders that the sick man should be seized and punished, but although a price was placed on his head, and he was searched for far and wide, he could never be caught. A clue to this is furnished by a passage in the *Lalita Vistara*. The sick man was in reality one of the Spirits of the Pure Abode, masquerading in sores and spasms. These Spirits of the Pure Abode are also called the Buddhas of the Past in many passages, as I shall shortly show.

Dr. Rhys Davids, in his translation of the Life of Buddha, calls them vaguely "angels," "fairies," etc.; but the whole question of early Buddhism is really bound up in the matter. In the Southern scriptures it is explained that the Spirits of the Pure Abode dwell in the heaven of Brahma.[1] I may mention too, that in a valuable inscription, copied from an old column in the island of Ceylon by Dr. Rhys Davids

[1] Turnour, *Journ. Beng. As. Soc.* vol. vii. p. 798.

himself, it is announced that in the reign of the king who erected it, the Buddha devatas "talked with men"[1] in the great temple. Here we have plainly the Buddhas of the past, of the *Lalita Vistara*. The disciples of the "Carriage which drives to the Great Nowhere" have senselessly interlarded this book with certain "Bodhisatwas of the Ten Regions," which, figuring side by side with the "Buddhas of the Ten Regions," confess the cheat. When the "Great Vehicle" movement dethroned the Buddhas of the past, it substituted Bodhisatwas (mortals who have reached the last stage of the metempsychosis), and transferred the old saint-worship, the sacrifices, processions, relic expositions, etc., to them.

For another valuable fact we are indebted to the Southern scriptures. They announce that the answers of the charioteer were given under inspiration from the unseen world.[2] On the surface this is plausible, for we shall see that the speeches of the charioteer were not always pitched in so high a key.

And it would almost seem as if some influence, malefic or otherwise, was stirring the good King Śuddhodana. Unmoved by failure, he urged the prince to a third effort. The chariot this time was to set out by the western gate. Greater precautions than ever were adopted. The chain of guards was posted at least twelve miles off from the Palace of Summer. But the Buddhas of the Ten Horizons again arrested the prince. His chariot was suddenly crossed by a phantom funeral procession. A phantom corpse, smeared with the orthodox mud, and spread with a sheet, was

[1] *Journ. As. Soc.* vol. vii. p. 364.
[2] Spence Hardy, *Manual*, p. 157.

carried on a bier. Phantom women wailed, and phantom musicians played on the drum and the Indian flute. No doubt also, phantom Brahmins chanted hymns to Jâtavedas, to bear away the immortal part of the dead man to the home of the Pitris.

"What is this?" said the prince. "Why do these women beat their breasts and tear their hair? Why do these good folks cover their heads with the dust of the ground. And that strange form upon its litter, wherefore is it so rigid?"

"Prince," said the charioteer, "this is Death! Yon form, pale and stiffened, can never again walk and move. Its owner has gone to the unknown caverns of Yama. His father, his mother, his child, his wife cry out to him, but he cannot hear."

Buddha was sad.

"Woe be to youth, which is the sport of age! Woe be to health, which is the sport of many maladies! Woe be to life, which is as a breath! Woe be to the idle pleasures which debauch humanity! But for the 'five aggregations' there would be no age, sickness, nor death. Go back to the city. I must compass the deliverance."

A fourth time the prince was urged by his father to visit the Garden of Happiness. The chain of guards this time was sixteen miles away. The exit was by the northern gate. But suddenly a calm man of gentle mien, wearing an ochre-red cowl, was seen in the roadway.

"Who is this," said the prince, "rapt, gentle, peaceful in mien? He looks as if his mind were far away elsewhere. He carries a bowl in his hand."

"Prince, this is the New Life," said the charioteer.

"That man is of those whose thoughts are fixed on the eternal Brahma [Brahmacharin]. He seeks the divine voice. He seeks the divine vision. He carries the alms-bowl of the holy beggar [bhikshu]. His mind is calm because the gross lures of the lower life can vex it no more."

"Such a life I covet," said the prince. "The lusts of man are like the sea-water—they mock man's thirst instead of quenching it. I will seek the divine vision, and give immortality to man!"

In the *Lalita Vistara* the remedy for age, sickness, and death is immortality.[1] In Dr. Rhys Davids' *Buddhism* the remedy for death is death. If the apologue was composed outside of Bedlam, it is plain that the *Lalita Vistara* gives us the correct version. If a prick with a dagger is the amṛita, why go through all the tortures of yoga to gain it?

King Śuddhodana was beside himself. He placed five hundred corseleted Śâkyas at every gate of the Palace of Summer. Chains of sentries were round the walls, which were raised and strengthened. A phalanx of loving wives, armed with javelins, was posted round the prince's bed to "narrowly watch" him. The king ordered also all the allurements of sense to be constantly presented to the prince.

"Let the women of the zenana cease not for an instant their concerts and mirth and sports. Let them shine in silks and sparkle in diamonds and emeralds."

Mahâ Prajâpatî, the aunt who since Queen Mâyâ's death has acted as foster-mother, has charge of these pretty young women, and she incites them to encircle the prince in a "cage of gold."

[1] "Un fruit de vie, de bien être, et d'immortalité" (Foucaux, p. 185).

The allegory is in reality a great battle between two camps—the denizens of the Kâmaloca, or the Domains of Appetite, and the denizens of the Brahmaloca, the Domains of pure Spirit. The latter are unseen, but not unfelt.

For one day, when the prince reclined on a silken couch listening to the sweet crooning of four or five brown-skinned, large-eyed Indian girls, his eyes suddenly assumed a dazed and absorbed look, and the rich hangings and garlands and intricate trellis-work of the golden apartment were still, present, but dim to his mind. And music and voices, more sweet than he had ever listened to, seemed faintly to reach him. I will write down some of the verses he heard, as they contain the mystic inner teaching of Buddhism.

'Mighty prop of humanity
March in the pathway of the Ṛishis of old,
Go forth from this city!
Upon this desolate earth,
When thou hast acquired the priceless knowledge of the Jinas,
When thou hast become a perfect Buddha,
Give to all flesh the baptism (river) of the Kingdom of Righteousness.
Thou who once didst sacrifice thy feet, thy hands, thy precious body, and all thy riches for the world,
Thou whose life is pure, save flesh from its miseries!
In the presence of reviling be patient, O conqueror of self!
Lord of those who possess two feet, go forth on thy mission!
Conquer the evil one and his army."

Thus run some more of these gâthâs :—

"Light of the world! [lamp du monde—Foucaux],
In former kalpas this vow was made by thee:
'For the worlds that are a prey to death and sickness I will be a refuge!'

Lion of men, master of those that walk on two feet, the time for thy mission has come!

Under the sacred Bo-tree acquire immortal dignity, and give Amṛita (immortality) to all!

When thou wert a king (in a former existence), and a subject insolently said to thee: 'These lands and cities, give them to me!'

Thou wert rejoiced and not troubled.

Once when thou wert a virtuous Ṛishi, and a cruel king in anger hacked off thy limbs, in thy death agony milk flowed from thy feet and thy hands.

When thou didst dwell on a mountain as the Ṛishi Syama, a king having transfixed thee with poisoned arrows, didst thou not forgive this king?

When thou wert the king of antelopes, didst thou not save thine enemy the hunter from a torrent?

When thou wert an elephant and a hunter pierced thee, thou forgavest him, and didst reward him with thy beautiful tusks!

Once when thou wert a she-bear thou didst save a man from a torrent swollen with snow. Thou didst feed him on roots and fruit until he grew strong;

And when he went away and brought back men to kill thee, thou forgavest him!

Once when thou wert the white horse,[1]
In pity for the suffering of man,
Thou didst fly across heaven to the region of the evil demons,
To secure the happiness of mankind.
Persecutions without end,
Revilings and many prisons,
Death and murder,
These hast thou suffered with love and patience,
Forgiving thine executioners.
Kingless, men seek thee for a king!
Stablish them in the way of Brahma and of the ten virtues,
That when they pass away from amongst their fellow-men, they may all go to the abode of Brahma."

---

[1] Yearly the sun-god as the zodiacal horse (Aries) was supposed by the Vedic Âryans to die to save all flesh. Hence the horse-sacrifice.

"By these gâthâs the prince is exhorted," says the narrative. And whilst the Jinas sing, beautiful women, with flowers and perfumes, and jewels and rich dresses, try to incite him to mortal love.

But to bring about their plans more quickly, the Spirits of the Pure Abode have conceived a new project. The beautiful women of the zenana are the main seductions of Mâra, the tempter, whom philologists prove to be closely connected with Kâma, the god of love. The Spirits of the Pure Abode determine that the prince shall see these women in a new light. By a subtle influence they induce him to visit the apartments of the women at the moment that they, the Jinas, have put all these women into a sound sleep.

Everything is in disorder — the clothes of the women, their hair, their trinkets. Some are lolling ungracefully on couches, some have hideous faces, some cough, some laugh sillily in their dreams, some rave. Also deformities and blemishes that female art had been careful to conceal are now made prominent by the superior magic of the spirits. This one has a discoloured neck, this one an ill-formed leg, this one a clumsy fat arm. Smiles have become grins, and fascinations a naked hideousness. Sprawling on couches in ungainly attitudes, all lie amidst their tawdry finery, their silent tambourines and lutes.

"Of a verity I am in a graveyard!" said the prince in great disgust.

And now comes an incident which is odd in the life of a professed atheist. Buddha has determined to leave the palace altogether. "Then he (Buddha) uncrossed his legs, and turning his eyes towards the eastern horizon, he put aside the precious trellis-work and repaired to the roof of the palace. Then joining the ten fingers of his hands, he thought of all the Buddhas and rendered homage to all the Buddhas, and, looking across the skies, he saw the Master of all the gods, he of the ten hundred eyes [Daśaśata Ṇayana]." Plainly he prayed to Indra. The Romantic Life also retains this incident, but it omits Indra, and makes Buddha pray only to all the Buddhas.

At the moment that Buddha joined his hands in homage towards the eastern horizon, the star Pushya, which had presided at his birth, was rising. The prince on seeing it said to Chandaka:

"The benediction that is on me has attained its perfection this very night. Give me at once the king of horses covered with jewels!"

The highest spiritual philosophers in Buddhism, in Brahminism, in Christendom, in Islam, announce two kingdoms distinct from one another. They are called in India the Domain of Appetite (Kâmaloca), and the Domain of Spirit (Brahmaloca). The *Lalita Vistara* throughout describes a conflict between these two great camps. Buddha is offered a crown by his father. He has wives, palaces, jewels, but he leaves all for the thorny jungle where the Brahmacharin dreamt his dreams of God. This is called pessimism by some writers, who urge that we should enjoy life as we find it, but modern Europe having tried, denies that life is so enjoyable. Its motto is *Tout lasse, tout casse, tout passe.* Yes, say the optimists, but we needn't all live a life like Jay Gould. A good son, a good father, a good husband, a good citizen, is happy enough. True, reply the pessimists, in so far as a mortal enters the domain of spirit he may be happy, for that is not a region but a state of the mind. But mundane accidents seem, almost by rule, to mar even that happiness. The husband loses his loved one, the artist his eyesight. Philosophers and statesmen find their great dreams and schemes baffled by the infirmities of age.

Age, disease, death! These are the evils for which the great Indian allegory proposes to find a remedy.

The Buddhas of the Past win the victory in spite of the fact that King Śuddhodana offers to resign the crown to his son if he will abandon the idea of a religious life. Buddha steals away one night on his horse Kantaka and enlists as a disciple of a Brahmin named Arâta Kâlâma. But by and by, becoming dissatisfied with his teacher, he retires to the silences of Buddha Gayâ and the famous Bo-tree. There occurs his celebrated conflict with Mâra, the Buddhist Satan, who comes in person to tempt him. Two of the temptations are precisely similar to those of Jesus. Buddha is said to have gone through a forty-nine days' fast, and the first temptation appeals to his hunger. For the second he is transported to the neighbourhood of the splendid city of Kapilavastu, which is made to revolve, like the "wheel of a potter," and display its magnificence.[1] The third temptation introduces a prominent feature in a fasting ascetic's visions. Beautiful females, the daughters of Mâra, come round him. But Buddha triumphs over them, and triumphs over their father, and by and by baptizes both.

For six years the ascetic sate under his Tree of Knowledge, the *pippala*, or *Ficus religiosa*. Then

[1] Bigandet's *Life of Buddha*, p. 65.

Brahma urges him to go and preach the *Brahmacharya*, the Knowledge of Brahma. It is called also the Glad Tidings, *Subhashita*.[1] He goes off to the celebrated deer forest of Benares and begins to make converts, using the actual words of Christ, "Follow Me!"

[1] On this point see Rajendra L. Mitra, *Northern Buddhist Literature*, p. 29.

CHAPTER IV

THE "WISDOM OF THE OTHER BANK"

If the Roman Catholics were told that St. François de Salis, or St. Jerome, "altogether ignored in nature any spiritual aspirations,"[1] they would feel a little astonished. This is the view taken of Buddha by the Boden Professor of Sanskrit at Oxford. And yet the word "Buddha" means, he who has attained the complete spiritual awakening. And Buddha's *Dharma* has for an alternative exponent the words *Prajñâ Pâramitâ* (the Wisdom of the Other Bank).

There are two states of the soul, call them ego and non-ego—the plane of matter and the plane of spirit,—what you will. As long as we live for the ego and its greedy joys, we are feverish, restless, miserable. Happiness consists in the destruction of the ego by the Bodhi, or Gnosis. This is that interior, that high state of the soul, attained by Fenelon and Wesley, by Mirza the Sufi and Swedenborg, by Spinoza and Amiel.

"The kingdom of God is within you," says Christ.

"In whom are hid the treasures of *sophia* and *gnosis*," says St. Paul.

"The enlightened view both worlds," says Mirza the Sufi, "but the bat flieth about in the darkness without seeing."

[1] Sir Monier Monier-Williams, *Buddhism*, p. 149.

"Who speaks and acts with the inner quickening," says Buddha, "has joy for his accompanying shadow. Who speaks and acts without the inner quickening, him sorrow pursues as the chariot-wheel the horse."

Let us give here a pretty parable, and let Buddha speak for himself:

"Once upon a time there was a man born blind, and he said, 'I cannot believe in a world of appearances. Colours bright or sombre exist not. There is no sun, no moon, no stars. None have witnessed such things.' His friends chid him; but he still repeated the same words.

"In those days there was a Ṛishi who had the inner vision; and he detected on the steeps of the lofty Himalayas four simples that had the power to cure the man who was born blind. He culled them, and, mashing them with his teeth, applied them. Instantly the man who was born blind cried out, 'I see colours and appearances. I see beautiful trees and flowers. I see the bright sun. No one ever saw like this before.'

"Then certain holy men came to the man who was born blind, and said to him, 'You are vain and arrogant, and nearly as blind as you were before. You see the outside of things, not the inside. One whose supernatural senses are quickened sees the lapis-lazuli fields of the Buddhas of the Past, and hears heavenly conch shells sounded at a distance of five yoganas. Go off to a desert, a forest, a cavern in the mountains, and conquer this mean thirst of earthly things.'"

The man who was born blind obeyed; and the parable ends with its obvious interpretation. Buddha is the old Ṛishi, and the four simples are the four great truths. He weans mankind from the lower life and opens the eyes of the blind.

I think that Sir Monier Monier-Williams' fancy, that Buddha ignored the spiritual side of humanity, is due to the fact that by the word "knowledge" he conceives the Buddhists to mean knowledge of material facts. That Buddha's conceptions are nearer to the ideas of Swedenborg than of Mill is, I think, proved by the Cingalese book, the Samanna Phala Sutta. Buddha details, at considerable length, the practices of the ascetic, and then enlarges upon their exact object. Man has a body composed of the four elements. It is the fruit of the union of his father and mother. It is nourished on rice and gruel, and may be truncated, crushed, destroyed. In this transitory body his intelligence is enchained. The ascetic, finding himself thus confined, directs his mind to the creation of a freer integument. He represents to himself in thought another body created from this material body—a body with a form, members, and organs. This body, in relation to the material body, is like the sword and the scabbard, or a serpent issuing from a basket in which it is confined. The ascetic, then, purified and perfected, commences to practise supernatural faculties. He finds himself able to pass through material obstacles, walls, ramparts, etc.; he is able to throw his phantasmal appearance into many places at once; he is able to walk upon the surface of water without immersing himself; he can fly through the air like a falcon furnished with large wings; he can leave this world and reach even the heaven of Brahma himself.

Another faculty is now conquered by his force of

will, as the fashioner of ivory shapes the tusk of the elephant according to his fancy. He acquires the power of hearing the sounds of the unseen world as distinctly as those of the phenomenal world—more distinctly, in point of fact. Also by the power of Manas he is able to read the most secret thoughts of others, and to tell their characters. He is able to say, "There is a mind that is governed by passion. There is a mind that is enfranchised. This man has noble ends in view. This man has no ends in view." As a child sees his earrings reflected in the water, and says, "Those are my earrings," so the purified ascetic recognises the truth. Then comes to him the faculty of "divine vision," and he sees all that men do on earth and after they die, and when they are again reborn. Then he detects the secrets of the universe, and why men are unhappy, and how they may cease to be so.

I will now quote a conversation between Buddha and some Brahmins which, I think, throws much light on his teaching. It is given in another Cingalese book, the *Tevigga Sutta.*

When Buddha was dwelling at Manasâkata in the mango grove, certain Brahmins learned in the three Vedas come to consult him on the question of union with the eternal Brahma. They ask if they are in the right pathway towards that union. Buddha replies at great length. He suggests an ideal case. He supposes that a man has fallen in love with the "most beautiful woman in the land." Day and night he dreams of her, but has never seen her. He does not know whether she is tall or short, of Brahmin or Śûdra caste, of dark or fair complexion; he does not even know her name. The Brahmins are asked if the talk of that man about that woman be wish or foolish. They confess that it is "foolish talk." Buddha then applies the same train of reasoning to them. The Brahmins versed in the three Vedas are made to confess that they have never seen Brahma, that they do not know whether he is tall or short, or anything about him, and that all their talk about union with him is also foolish talk. They are mounting a crooked staircase, and do not know whether it leads to a mansion or a precipice. They are standing on the bank of a river and calling to the other bank to come to them.

Now it seems to me that if Buddha were the uncompromising teacher of atheism that many folks picture him, he has at this point an admirable opportunity of urging his views. The Brahmins, he would of course contend, knew nothing about Brahma, for the simple reason that no such being as Brahma exists.

But this is exactly the line that Buddha does not take. His argument is that the Brahmins knew nothing of Brahma, because Brahma is purely spiritual, and they are purely materialistic.

Five "Veils," he shows, hide Brahma from mortal ken. These are—

1. The Veil of Lustful Desire.
2. The Veil of Malice.
3. The Veil of Sloth and Idleness.
4. The Veil of Pride and Self-righteousness.
5. The Veil of Doubt.

Buddha then goes on with his questionings:

"Is Brahma in possession of wives and wealth?"

"He is not, Gautama!" answers Vâsettha the Brahmin.

"Is his mind full of anger, or free from anger?"

"Free from anger, Gautama!"

"Is his mind full of malice, or free from malice?"

"Free from malice, Gautama!"

"Is his mind depraved or pure?"

"It is pure, Gautama!"

"Has he self-mastery, or has he not?"

"He has, Gautama."

The Brahmins are then questioned about themselves.

"Are the Brahmins versed in the three Vedas, in possession of wives and wealth, or are they not?"

"They are, Gautama!"

"Have they anger in their hearts, or have they not?"

"They have, Gautama."

"Do they bear malice, or do they not?"

"They do, Gautama."

"Are they pure in heart, or are they not?"

"They are not, Gautama."

"Have they self-mastery, or have they not?"

"They have not, Gautama."

These replies provoke, of course, the very obvious retort that no point of union can be found between such dissimilar entities. Brahma is free from malice, sinless, self-contained, so, of course, it is only the sinless that can hope to be in harmony with him.

Vâsettha then puts this question: "It has been told me, Gautama, that Śramaṇa Gautama knows the way to the state of union with Brahma?"

"Brahma I know, Vâsettha!" says Buddha in reply, "and the world of Brahma, and the path leading to it!"

The humbled Brahmins learned in the three Vedas then ask Buddha to "show them the way to a state of union with Brahma."

Buddha replies at considerable length, drawing a sharp contrast between the lower Brahminism and the higher Brahminism, the "householder" and the "houseless one." The householder Brahmins are gross, sensual, avaricious, insincere. They practise for lucre black magic, fortune-telling, cozenage. They gain the ear of kings, breed wars, predict victories, sacrifice life, spoil the poor. As a foil to this he paints the recluse, who has renounced all worldly things and is pure, self-possessed, happy.

To teach this "higher life," a Tathâgata "from time to time is born into the world, blessed and worthy, abounding in wisdom, a guide to erring mortals." He sees the universe face to face, the spirit world of Brahma and that of Mâra the tempter. He makes his knowledge known to others. The houseless one, instructed by him, "lets his mind pervade one quarter of the world with thoughts of pity, sympathy, and equanimity; and so the second, and so the third, and so the fourth. And thus the whole wide world, above, below, around, and everywhere, does he continue to pervade with heart of pity, sympathy, and equanimity, far-reaching, grown great, and beyond measure."[1]

"Verily this, Vâsettha, is the way to a state of union with Brahma," and he proceeds to announce that the Bhikshu, or Buddhist beggar, "who is free from anger, free from malice, pure in mind, master of himself, will, after death, when the body is dissolved, become united with Brahma." The Brahmins at once see the full force of this teaching. It is as a conservative in their eyes that Buddha figures, and not an innovator. He

[1] Rhys Davids, *Buddhist Suttas*, p. 201.

takes the side of the ancient spiritual religion of the country against rapacious innovators.

"Thou hast set up what was thrown down," they say to him. In the Burmese Life he is described more than once as one who has set the overturned chalice once more upon its base.

The word *Dharma* means much in Buddhism.

"Obey the eternal law of the heavens. Who keeps this law lives happily in this world and the next.[1]

"For the enfranchised soul human suffering no longer exists.[2]

"In the darkness of this world few men see clearly. Very few soar heavenwards like a bird freed from a net."[3]

No doubt the discipline of extasia was expected to give vitality to this inner quickening. When actual visions of the Buddhas of the ten regions were before the eyes of the fasting visionary, it was judged that he would have a more practical belief in their lapis-lazuli domains. The heart of the Eastern nations has been truer to its great teacher than their learned metaphysicians have been. The epoch of Buddha is called the "Era when the Milken Rice [immortality] came into the world."[4] This certainty of a heavenly kingdom was not to be confined, as in the orthodox Brahminism, to a priestly caste. A king had become a beggar that he might preach to beggars. In the Chinese *Dhammapada* there is a pretty story of a very beautiful Magdalen who had heard of Buddha, and who started off to hear him preach. On the way, however, she saw her beautiful face in a fountain near

[1] *Dhammapada*, v. 169.
[2] *Ibid.* v. 90.
[3] *Ibid.* v. 174.
[4] Upham, *Hist. Buddhism*, p. 48.

which she stopped to drink, and she was unable to carry out her good resolution. As she was returning she was overtaken by a courtesan still more beautiful than herself, and they journeyed together. Resting for awhile at another fountain, the beautiful stranger was overcome with sleep, and placed her head on her fellow-traveller's lap. Suddenly the beautiful face became livid as a corpse, loathsome, a prey to hateful insects. The stranger was the great Buddha himself, who had put on this appearance to redeem poor Puṇḍarî.[1] "There is a loveliness that is like a beautiful jar full of filth, a beauty that belongs to eyes, nose, mouth, body. It is this womanly beauty that causes sorrow, divides families, kills children." These words, uttered by the great teacher on another occasion, were perhaps retailed a second time for the Buddhist Magna Civitatis Peccatrix.[2]

The penitent thief, too, is to be heard of in Buddhism. Buddha confronts a cruel bandit in his mountain retreat and converts him.[3] All great movements, said St. Simon, must begin by working on the emotion of the masses.

Another originality of the teaching of Buddha was the necessity of individual effort. Ceremonial, sacrifice, the exertions of others, could have no possible effect on any but themselves. Against the bloody sacrifice of the Brahmins he was specially remorseless.

"How can the system which requires the infliction of misery on others be called a religious system? . . . How having a body defiled with blood will the shedding

[1] Chinese *Dhammapada*, p. 35. [2] *Ibid.* p. 159.
[3] *Ibid.* p. 48.

of blood restore it to purity? To seek a good by doing an evil is surely no safe plan!"[1]

Even a Buddha could only show the sinner the right path. "Tathâgatas are only preachers. You yourself must make an effort."[2]

Buddha's theology made another great advance on other creeds, a step which our century is only now attempting to overtake. He strongly emphasised the remorseless logic of cause and effect in the deteriorating influence of evil actions on the individual character. The Judas of Buddhism, Devadatta, repents and is forgiven. But Buddha cannot annul the causation of his evil deeds. These will have to be dealt with by slow degrees in the purgatorial stages of the hereafter. He knows no theory of a dull bigot on his deathbed suddenly waking up with all the broad sympathies and large knowledge of the angel Gabriel. Unless in the next life a being takes up his intellectual and moral condition exactly at the stage he left it in this, it is plain that logically his individuality is lost. This teaching of Buddha has been whimsically enforced by some of his followers. His own words are trenchant and clear: "A fault once committed is like milk, which grows not sour all at once. Patiently and silently, like a smothered ember, shall it inch by inch devour the fool."[3] "Both a good action and an evil action must ripen and bear their inevitable fruit."[4]

This teaching has been powerfully inculcated in one oı two fine parables, in which the consequences of sin are imaged as an iron city of torment, and the sins themselves figure as beautiful women luring man to his

[1] *Romantic History*, p. 159.
[2] *Dhammapada*, v. 276.
[3] *Ibid.* v. 71.
[4] Burnouf, Introd. p. 87.

ruin. On the surface all is as bewitching as a scene of the *Arabian Nights*. The palm-trees of a soft island rustle gently, and in a delicious palace the mean seeker of gold, the bad son, is fanned by women of a beauty unknown to earth. He has sought the unworthy prizes of the Kâmaloca, and he enjoys them for a time, because with Buddha the full basket and store of the Brahmin and the old Jew are not deemed the rewards of heaven, but of quite another region. From island to island the wanderer goes, each island being more delicious than the preceding one, but each being nearer to the iron-walled city of expiation. But the furies are cause and effect, and not an eternal Ahriman. There is no devil that Buddha cannot soften.[1]

This suggests another great advance made by Buddha. In his day the beneficent God was deemed the god of a nation, a tribe; and all the gods of other nations were deemed evil demons. This creed is the real "agnosticism" and "atheism," because its main postulate implies that the reason and conscience of humanity for thousands and thousands of years have been unable to discover God, and that if He has been found at all, it is to accident alone that the discovery is due; even if the discovered god should not upon examination be found to be composed of very poor clay. But the missionaries of Tathâgata were sent to every nation, and Buddha is the first historical teacher who proclaimed that even in the hell Avîchi was no recess sheltered from Tathâgata's all-pervading love.

But the crowning legacy to humanity of this priceless benefactor was his boundless compassion. "Buddha,"

[1] Beal, *Romantic History*. Comp. Story of the Five Hundred Merchants, p. 332, and the Merchant, p. 342.

say his disciples, "was God revealed in the form of Mercy." The theory that Buddha was a myth seems quite to break down here, for some such character must have existed, that ideas so far in advance even of modern days could have been conceived. His majestic gentleness never varies. He converts the Very Wicked One. He speaks gently to the Daughters of Sin. He clears out even the lowest of hells when he visits earth, and makes devils as well as good men happy. A fool outrages and insults him: "My son," he replies, "outrage addressed to heaven is like spittle aimed into the skies: it returns upon the author of the outrage."[1] And he explained to his disciples that Tathâgata could never be made angry by foul actions and invectives. Such can only make him redouble his mercy and love.[2] When we reflect that the principle of retaliation was the rude policy of the day in which he lived, and that aggregations of men were obliged to foster a love of revenge, war, plunder, and bloodshed in their midst, prompted by the mere instinct of self-preservation, such great sentences as the following of Buddha are indeed noteworthy:—

"By love alone can we conquer wrath. By good alone can we conquer evil. The whole world dreads violence. All men tremble in the presence of death. Do to others that which ye would have them do to you. Kill not. Cause no death."[3]

"Say no harsh words to thy neighbour. He will reply to thee in the same tone."[4]

"'I am injured and provoked, I have been beaten

[1] Sûtra of Forty-two Sections," sect. viii. [2] *Ibid.* sect. vii.

[3] *Ibid.* v. 129. M. Léon Feer gives here the very words of Luke vi. 31.

[4] *Ibid.* v. 133.

and plundered!' They who speak thus will never cease to hate."

"That which can cause hate to cease in the world is not hate, but the absence of hate."[1]

"If, like a trumpet trodden on in battle, thou complainest not, thou hast attained Nirvâṇa."

"Silently shall I endure abuse, as the war-elephant receives the shaft of the bowman."

"The awakened man goes not on revenge, but rewards with kindness the very being who has injured him, as the sandal-tree scents the axe of the woodman who fells it."[2]

I will now copy down a few miscellaneous sayings of Buddha:—

"The swans go on the path of the sun. They go through the air by means of their miraculous power. The wise are led out of this world when they have conquered Mâra and his train."[3]

"A man is not a Śramaṇa by outward acts."

"Not by tonsure does an undisciplined man become a Śramaṇa."

"There is no satisfying of lusts with a shower of gold pieces."

"A man is not a Bhikshu simply because he asks others for alms. A man is not a Muni because he observes silence. Not by discipline and vows, not by much spiritual knowledge, not by sleeping alone, not by the gift of holy inspiration, can I earn that release which no worldling can know. The real Śramaṇa is he who has quieted all evil."

[1] Sûtra of Forty-two Sections, v. 4, 5.

[2] This is claimed by the Brahmins likewise, but it is quite foreign to their genius. *Vide* Hodgson, *Essays*, p. 74.

[3] *Dhammapada.*

"If one man conquer in battle a thousand thousand men, and another conquer himself, the last is the greatest conqueror."

"Few are there amongst men who arrive at the other shore. Many run up and down the shore."

"Let the fool wish for a false reputation, for precedence amongst the Bhikshus, for lordship in the convents, for worship amongst other people."

"A supernatural person is not easily found. He is not born everywhere. Wherever such a sage is born that race prospers."

"Call not out in this way as if I were the god Brahma" (Chinese parable).

"Religion is nothing but the faculty of love."[1]

"The house of Brahma is that wherein children obey their parents."[2]

"The elephant's cub, if he find not leafless and thorny creepers in the greenwood, becomes thin."[3]

"Beauty and riches are like a knife smeared with honey. The child sucks and is wounded."[4]

The One Thing Needful

Certain subtle questions were proposed to Buddha, such as: What will best conquer the evil passions of man? What is the most savoury gift for the alms-bowl of the mendicant? Where is true happiness to be found? Buddha replied to them all with one word, *Dharma*[5] (the heavenly life).

I will now give some of the Buddhist parables, some almost unequalled for beauty.

[1] Bigandet, p. 223.
[2] Burnouf, Introd.
[3] Hodgson, p. 74.
[4] Sûtra of Forty-two Sections, sect. xxi.
[5] Bigandet, p. 225.

CHAPTER V

PARABLES

THE PARABLE OF THE FORGIVENESS OF INJURIES

IN a previous existence Buddha was once the ascetic Jin Juh, and he dwelt in a forest. "Forests are delightful," he subsequently declared. "Where the worldling finds no delight, there the awakened man will find delight." At this time there was a king called Ko Li, who was possessed of a cruel and wicked disposition. One day, taking his women with him, he entered the forest to hunt, and becoming tired, he lay down to sleep. Then all the women went into the woods to gather flowers, and they came to the cell of the ascetic Jin Juh, and listened to his teaching. After some time the king awoke, and having missed the women, he became jealous, and drew his sword, and went in search of them. Seeing them all standing in front of the cell of the ascetic, he became very angry indeed.

"Who are you?" he said.

"I am the ascetic Jin Juh!"

"Have you conquered all earthly passions?" pursued the king.

The ascetic replied that he was there to struggle with passion.

"If you have not attained Sheung te teng," said the

king, "I do not see that you are better than the philosophers [Fan fuh]"; and with the cruelty of an Eastern tyrant, he hacked off the hands and feet of the poor hermit.

Perceiving a majestic calm still upon the face of the tortured ascetic, the astonished monarch asked him if he felt no anger.

"None, king, and I will one day teach thee also to curb thy wild-beast passions. When, in another existence, I attain Sheung te teng [Nirvâṇa], thou, O king, shalt be my first convert."

In a subsequent existence King Ko Li became the disciple Kaundiliya.

In the next parable we get, I think, a protest of the Little Vehicle against the "false teachers" of the innovating school.

The Parable of the Atheist

Angati, a king in Tirhut, had a daughter, Ruchî. At first he lived piously, but one day he heard some false teachers who declared that there is no future world, and that man, after death, is resolved into water and the other elements. After this he thought it was better to enjoy the present moment, and he became cruel.

One day Ruchî went to the king and requested him to give her one thousand gold pieces, as the next day was a festival and she wished to make an offering. The king replied that there was no future world, no reward for merit; religious rites were useless, and it was better to enjoy herself in the present world.

Now Ruchî possessed the inner vision, and was able to trace back her life through fourteen previous existences. She told the king that she had once been a nobleman, but an adulterer, and as a punishment she was now only a woman. As a further punishment she had been a monkey, a bullock, a goat, and had been once born into the hell Avîchi. The king, unwilling to be taught by a woman, continued to be a sceptic. Ruchî then, by the power of an incantation, summoned a spirit to her aid, and Buddha himself, in the form of an ascetic, arrived at the city. The king asked him from whence he came. The ascetic replied that he came from the other world. The king, in answer, laughingly said:

"If you have come from the other world, lend me one hundred gold pieces, and when I go to that world I will give you a thousand."

Buddha answered gravely:

"When any one lends money, it must be to the rich. If he bestow money on the poor, it is a gift, for the poor cannot repay. I cannot lend you, therefore, one hundred gold pieces, for you are poor and destitute."

"You utter an untruth," said the king angrily. "Does not this rich city belong to me?"

The Buddha replied:

"In a short time, O king, you will die. Can you take your wealth with you to hell? There you will be in unspeakable misery, without raiment, without food. How, then, can you pay me my debt?"

At this moment on the face of Buddha was a strange light which dazzled the king. Of the next story there are many versions. It is very popular in Buddhist countries.

Buddha's Parable of Kîsogotamî

Once a humble couple lived at Śrâvastî. They sold pulse, rice, and charcoal, laid out in little round flat baskets, with a bit of poor matting propped up on bamboos to keep off the midday sun. They had an only daughter Kîsogotamî. One day her father sent her to fetch some wood. She stayed in the jungle plucking flowers, until in a thicket she suddenly saw the fierce eyes of a cheetah staring at her. She very nearly died of fright. Suddenly something whizzed by her and laid the cheetah dead at her feet. It was an arrow shot by a comely young hunter, a servant of the Râjah. He wanted soon after that to marry Kîsogotamî, who was very pretty, but the old parents said that they could not spare their only child. One day a blind man passed the little shop singing and playing on the vîṇâ. The old mother listened to his song—

> "Without a mate the Kokila grows silent on the spray,
> Silent—silent—silent soon for aye."

This led her to watch her daughter, who was really pining and very sick. In process of time, through the influence of the mother, the young girl was married. In those days a fierce tiger ravaged the district and killed many villagers. At once the Râjah offered a large reward for his destruction. The husband of Kîsogotamî lured by this attacked the tiger, but was clawed to death. The widow and a young child returned to Śrâvastî to meet, alas! a procession of wailing women accompanying her parents to the grave. A month after this the poor widow was seen carrying a dead child in her arms, and moaning piteously the words, "Give me some medicine for my suffering boy!"

One answered, "Go to Śâkya Muni, the Buddha!"

Kîsogotamî repaired to the cell of Buddha, and accosted him, "Lord and master, do you know of any medicine that will cure my boy?"

Buddha answered, "I want a handful of mustard-seed."

The girl promised to procure it, but Buddha added, "I require some mustard-seed taken from a house where no son, husband, parent, or slave has died."

Poor Kîsogotamî, with the dead child carried astride of her hip in the Indian fashion, went from house to house. The compassionate people said, "Here is mustard-seed, take it!" But when she asked if any son, or husband, or parent, or slave had died in that house, she received for a reply, "Lady, the living are few, the dead are many; death comes to every house!" At last, weary and hopeless, Kîsogotamî sat down by the wayside, and watched the lamps of the city being extinguished one by one. At this instant Buddha, by the power of Siddhi, placed his phantasm before her, which said to her, "All living beings resemble those lamps. They are lit up and flicker for awhile, and then dark night reigns over all." The appearance then preached the law to her, and, in the words of the Chinese version, he provided "salvation and refuge, pointing out the path that leads to the eternal city."

The Story of Prince Kunâla

King Aśoka had an infant boy whose eyes were so beautiful that his father called him Kunâla. There is a bird of this name that dwells amongst the rhododendrons and pines of the Himalayas. It is famed for its lovely eyes. The young prince grew up. His beauty was the talk of the king's dominions. No woman could gaze into his eyes without falling in love with him. A Buddhist Sthavira (*lit.* old man) spoke serious words to him one day: "The pride of the eye, my son, is vanity! Beware!"

At an early age Kunâla married a young girl, named Kâñchana. One day a royal lady saw the young husband, and fell desperately in love with his fine eyes. Kunâla was horrorstruck at this.

"Are you not," he said, "in the zenana of the king, my father?" This speech changed her love to a bitter hate.

At this time the city of Taxila revolted against King Aśoka. The monarch desired to hasten thither, but his ministers counselled him to send Prince Kunâla in his place. The prince repaired to the revolted city and soon restored quiet. The people assured him that it was the exactions and oppressions of the king's officers that they had resisted, not the king himself.

Soon the king became afflicted with a revolting malady, and wanted to abdicate in favour of his son. The Queen Tishya Rakshitâ, she who hated the prince, thought in her heart, "If Kunâla mounts the throne, I am lost!" She ordered her slaves to bring her a man afflicted with the same malady as the king. She poisoned this man and had his inside examined. A huge worm was feeding upon it. She fed this worm with pepper and with ginger. The worm was none the worse. She fed it with onion, it died.

Immediately she repaired to the king and promised to cure him if he would grant her a boon. The king promised to grant her anything she asked him. She said to him, "Take this onion and you will be well."

"Queen," said the king, "I am a Kshatriya, and the laws of Manu[1] forbid me to eat onion." The queen told him it was medicine, not food. He ate the onion and was cured.

The boon demanded by the queen as a recompense for this great cure was a week's rule of the king's dominions. The king hesitated, but was over-persuaded. Immediately the queen sent an order sealed with the royal seal that Prince Kunâla should be forced to wear the garments of a beggar and have both his eyes put out. A blind prince cannot mount the throne.

The good folks of Taxila were thunderstruck at this command, but they said to each other, "If the king is so merciless to his son, what will he be to us if we disobey him!" Some low-caste Chaṇḍâlas were summoned; they loved the prince, and would not execute the cruel order. At last a hideous object, a man deformed and stained with eighteen unsightly marks, came forward and tore out the prince's eyes. Soon he found himself a beggar on the high-road. His wife, Kâñchana, also clad in rags, was by his side. The poor prince now remembered the solemn words of the Sthavira.

"The outside world," he said to his wife, "is it not a mere globe of flesh?"

The prince had always been sickly, and to support himself now he played upon an instrument called the vîṇâ. After many wanderings they reached Palibothra (Patna), and approached the palace of the king; but the guards, seeing two dirty beggars, thrust them out summarily.

[1] Mânava Dharma Śâstra, iv. st. 5.

By and by the king heard the sound of the vîṇâ.

"It is my son," he said. He sent out officers of the court to bring him in. His condition filled the king with amazement. When he understood what had happened he summoned the guilty queen to his presence and ordered her to be burnt alive.

But the Prince Kunâla was now a changed man. When he felt himself deserted, as he thought, by his earthly father, he had become a son of Buddha (fils de Buddha).[1] His "eye of flesh" had been put out, but he felt that the spiritual vision had been for the first time awakened. In lieu of the soft clothes of Kaśi, he now wore the rags of one of Buddha's sublime beggars. He threw himself at the feet of his father, and pleaded for the queen's life: "I feel no anger, no pain, only gratitude. Kill her not."

Aśoka, the powerful sun-king, was destined to rule India with a sway more extensive than that of the proudest Mogul. He was destined also to abandon his luxurious palaces, and himself wander along the highway begging his food. He too became a Bhikshu.

A Buddha at a Marriage Feast

King Sudarsana was a model king. In his dominions was no killing or whipping as punishment; no soldiers' weapons to torture or destroy. His city, Jambunada, was built of crystal and cornelian, and silver and yellow gold. A Buddha visited it one day.

Now in that city was a man who was the next day to be married, and he much wished the Buddha to

[1] Burnouf, Introd. pp. 365, 366.

come to the feast. Buddha, passing by, read his silent wish, and consented to come. The bridegroom was overjoyed, and scattered many flowers over his house and sprinkled it with perfumes.

The next day Buddha, with his alms-bowl in his hand and with a retinue of many followers, arrived; and when they had taken their seats in due order, the host distributed every kind of exquisite food, saying, "Eat, my lord, and all the congregation, according to your desire!"

But now a marvel presented itself to the astonished mind of the host. Although all these holy men ate very heartily, the meats and the drinks remained positively quite undiminished; whereupon he argued in his mind, "If I could only invite all my kinsmen to come, the banquet would be sufficient for them likewise."

And now another marvel was presented. Buddha read the good man's thought, and all the relatives without invitation streamed in at the door. They, also, fed heartily on the miraculous food. It is almost needless to add that the Chinese book *Fu-pen-hing-tsi-king* (as translated by the invaluable Mr. Beal) announces that all these guests, having heard a few apposite remarks on Dharma from the lips of the Tathâgata, to the satisfaction of everybody (excepting, perhaps, the poor bride), donned the yellow robes.

The next parable is a very pretty one, and shows that a love that can pierce the limits of this narrow world and range amongst the Devalokas of the hereafter could be conceived even in the age of Śâkya Muni.

THE STORY OF THE GIRL BHADRÂ

When Śâkya Muni was in a previous existence, a certain King Sûryapati invited the great Buddha Dîpañkara to visit his dominions; and to do him honour he issued an edict that all his subjects within a radius of twelve yoganas from his chief city should reserve all flowers and perfume for the king and his offerings to the Buddha. No one was to be in possession of these offerings on his own account.

Śâkya was at this time a young Brahmin named Megha. He was well versed in the law, although he was only sixteen years of age. He was incomparable in appearance; his body like yellow gold, and his hair the same. His voice was as soft and sweet as the voice of Brahma. He happened to reach the city at the very moment that it was adorned in expectation of the coming of the Buddha Dîpañkara, and having already vague yearnings after the Buddhaship in his breast, he determined to make an offering to the incarnate Buddha.

He reasoned thus in his heart: "What offering shall I make to him? Buddhas contemn offerings of money; I will purchase the most beautiful flower I can find."

He went to a hairdresser's shop and selected a lovely flower, but the hairdresser refused to sell it. "The king has given orders, respectable youth, that no chaplets of flowers in this city are on any account to be sold!" Megha went off to a second and then to a third hairdresser's shop, and was met everywhere with the same refusal.

Now, it happened that, as he was pursuing his

search, he saw a dark-clad water-girl, whose name was Bhadrâ, secretly take a seven-stalked Utpala flower and put it inside her water-pitcher, and then go on her way. Megha went up to her and accosted her. "What are you going to do with that Utpala flower which I saw you put into your pitcher? I will give you five hundred gold pieces for it if you will sell it to me."

The young girl was arrested by the novel appearance of the handsome young man. She answered presently, "Beautiful youth, have you not heard that the great Dîpañkara Buddha is now about to enter the city in consequence of the king's invitation, and the king has issued orders that whatsoever scented unguents or flowers there are within twelve yoganas of the city are not on any account to be sold to any private individual, as the king will buy them all up for the purpose of presenting them to the Buddha. Now, in our neighbourhood there is a certain hair-dresser's wife, who privately took from me five hundred pieces of money and gave me in return this seven-stalked flower; and the reason why I have thus transgressed the edict of the king is, that I want myself to make an offering to the holy man."

Then Megha answered, "My good girl, what you have said will justify you in taking my five hundred gold pieces, and in giving me five stalks of the Utpala flower and reserving two for yourself."

She answered, "What will you do with the flowers if I give them to you?"

The young Brahmin told her that he wished to offer them to Buddha.

Now, it happened that this young girl was gifted

with the inner vision, and she knew from the youth's remarkable appearance that he was destined one day to become the guide of men. She said, "Fair stranger, one day you will be a great Buddha, and if you will promise me that, up to the day of your Buddhahood, at each new birth you will take me as your wife, and that when you attain Nirvâṇa you will let me follow you as a disciple in your retinue of followers, then will I give you five stalks of this Utpala flower."

The Brahmin replied that an ascetic was required to give all his wealth to his fellow-men, and that if she consented to such an arrangement he was willing to contract that she should ever be his wife. She sold to him five stalks of the Utpala flower, that they might be his own special gift to the Buddha, and she desired him to present the other two stalks as her own free gift.

When Dîpañkara approached, majestic and with a countenance like a glassy lake, the offering was thrown to him, and by a miracle the flowers remained in mid air, forming a canopy over his head.

Amongst the "Fan heavens" of the Chinese is one called Fuh-ngai (happy love). Let us hope that in that heaven the pretty Bhikshu Bhadrâ is still near her favourite teacher.

King Wessantara

Buddha once lived on earth as King Wessantara. So kind was he to everybody that it was rumoured that he had made a resolution to give to everybody whatever he was asked. He had a loving wife and two children. He had also an enchanted white elephant.

A grievous famine burst out in a neighbouring kingdom, and the poor died by thousands. Eight Brahmins were sent to King Wessantara to ask him for the white elephant; for fertile rain always falls in countries where an enchanted white elephant is staying. The benign king gave up his white elephant. This so incensed his own people that they deposed him.

Wessantara gave all his wealth to the poor, and departed in a carriage drawn by two horses, intending to repair to an immense rock in the wilderness, and there become a hermit. On his way he met two poor Brahmins, who asked him for his carriage. He complied, and the deposed king and queen, each carrying a child, made the rest of the journey on foot. Their road lay through the kingdom of the queen's father, who sought to overcome their resolution, but in vain.

Meanwhile a Brahmin named Jutaka was living very happily with a beautiful wife, until one day some envious neighbours poisoned her mind as she was drawing water at a well. They persuaded her she was a slave, and so incensed her that she attacked her husband and beat him and pulled his beard. Moreover, she threatened to leave his house unless he procured for her two slaves. A foolish king, she said, named Wessantara, was dwelling as a hermit in the wilderness; let him go there and ask for two slaves. He had two children, and had made a vow to refuse no one any demand.

Jutaka departed, but found all access to the royal

hermit denied by a hunter placed there by the queen's father, who, knowing Wessantara's vow, had desired to screen him from the further importunities of the greedy. Jutaka told him a lying tale and contrived to reach the hermit. He demanded the two children as slaves, and Wessantara was bound by his oath to hand them over to him. Jutaka, as soon as he was out of sight of the king, bound the royal children firmly with cords; but missing his way in the wilderness, came by chance to the territory of the queen's father, who was quickly apprised of all that had occurred.

He summoned the Brahmin before him, and offered him in exchange for the grandchildren the weight of them in gold pieces. The greedy Brahmin's end was not unlike that of Judas, for with his ill-gotten wealth he made a great feast, and from repletion his bowels also gushed out.[1]

King Bambadat

Buddha was in one of his births a merchant of Benares, and as he was one day passing with his wife in a carriage through the streets of Râjâgṛiha, the capital of King Bambadat, the monarch saw his wife and became captivated with her unrivalled beauty.

Immediately he hatched an infamous plot to gain her. He sent one of his officers to drop furtively a jewel of great value in the merchant's carriage. The poor merchant was then arrested on the charge

[1] This parable and the two following are given by Upham from the Jâtakas of the Buddha.

of stealing the royal gem. He and his beautiful wife were brought before the king, who listened to the evidence with mock attention, and then ordered the merchant to be executed and his wife to be detained in the royal harem. King Bambadat was a cruel monarch, whose oppressions had earned him the hatred of his subjects.

The poor merchant was led away to be decapitated, but Indra on his throne in heaven had witnessed the atrocious transaction; and, lo! a miracle was accomplished. As the executioner raised his sword, the king, who was watching the bloody event, was suddenly made to change places with the merchant by the agency of unseen hands, and he received the fatal blow; whilst Buddha suddenly found himself exalted on the royal elephant that had brought the king to the spot. This striking interposition of Heaven awed the assembled populace, and they proclaimed the merchant their new king. It is needless to add that his rule formed a striking contrast to that of King Bambadat. It is not mentioned, but I think it is very plain also, that the beautiful wife was the girl Bhadrâ of the former story. Buddhism has done much evil by its enforced sacerdotal celibacy, but, on the other hand, it seems to have had the honour of first conceiving a love of man with woman that could pierce the skies and be prolonged after death.

The Hungry Dog

There was once a wicked king named Usuratanam who oppressed his people so much that Buddha from the sky took compassion upon them. At this time he was the god Indra, and, assuming the form of a huntsman, he came down to earth with the Deva Mâtali, disguised as a dog of enormous size. They at once entered the palace of the king, and the dog barked so wofully that the sound seemed to shake the royal buildings to their very foundations. The king, affrighted, had the hunter brought before him; and he inquired the portent of these terrible sounds.

"It is through hunger that the dog barks," said the huntsman, and again a sound louder far than thunder reverberated through the palace.

"Fetch him food! Fetch anything!" cried the king in terror. All the food that happened then to be prepared was the royal banquet. It was placed before the dog. He ate it with surprising rapidity, and then barked once more with his terrible voice. More food was sent for, the food stored up in the city, the food of the adjacent provinces, but still the insatiable dog, after a brief interval, ate all up and barked for more. The king could scarcely prevent himself from falling to the earth with terror.

"Will nothing ever satisfy your dog, O hunter?"

"Nothing, O king, but the flesh of all his enemies."

"And who are his enemies, O hunter?"

"His enemies," said the hunter, "are those who do wicked deeds, who oppress the poor, who make war, who are cruel to the brute creation."

The king, remembering his many evil deeds, was seized with terror and remorse; and the Buddha, revealing himself, preached the law of righteousness to him and his people. It is plain that in the original story, as in the last, Indra alone was the supernatural agent, and the clumsy introduction of Buddha is an afterthought. Mâtali is the conventional charioteer of Indra, which, I think, is an additional proof.

Buddha as a Peacemaker

It is recorded that two princes were once about to engage in a terrible battle in a quarrel that took place about a certain embankment constructed to keep in water. Between these kings and their assembled armies Buddha suddenly appeared and asked the cause of the strife. When he was completely informed upon the subject, he put the following questions:

"Tell me, O kings! is earth of any intrinsic value?"

"Of no value whatever," was the reply.

"Is water of any intrinsic value?"

"Of no value whatever!"

"And the blood of kings, is that of any intrinsic value?"

"Its value is priceless!"

"Is it reasonable," asked the Tathâgata, "that that which is priceless should be staked against that which has no value whatever?"

The incensed monarchs saw the wisdom of this reasoning, and abandoned their dispute.[1]

The Prodigal Son[2]

A certain man had a son who went away into a far country. There he became miserably poor. The

[1] Bigandet, p. 191.
[2] This is the title adopted in the translation of M. Foucaux.

father, however, grew rich, and accumulated much gold and treasure, and many storehouses and elephants. But he tenderly loved his lost son, and secretly lamented that he had no one to whom to leave his palaces and suverṇas at his death.

After many years the poor man, in search of food and clothing, happened to come to the country where his father had great possessions. And when he was afar off his father saw him, and reflected thus in his mind: "If I at once acknowledge my son and give to him my gold and my treasures, I shall do him a great injury. He is ignorant and undisciplined; he is poor and brutalised. With one of such miserable inclinations, 'twere better to educate the mind little by little. I will make him one of my hired servants."

Then the son, famished and in rags, arrived at the door of his father's house; and, seeing a great throne upraised and many followers doing homage to him who sat upon it, was awed by the pomp and the wealth around. Instantly he fled once more to the highway. "This," he thought, "is the house of the poor man. If I stay at the palace of the king perhaps I shall be thrown into prison."

Then the father sent messengers after his son; who was caught and brought back in spite of his cries and lamentations. When he reached his father's house he fell down fainting with fear, not recognising his father, and believing that he was about to suffer some cruel punishment. The father ordered his servants to deal tenderly with the poor man, and sent two labourers of his own rank of life to engage him as a servant on the estate. They gave him a broom and a basket, and engaged him to clean up the dungheap at a double wage.

From the window of his palace the rich man watched his son at his work; and disguising himself one day as a poor man, and covering his limbs with dust and dirt, he approached his son and said, "Stay here, good man, and I will provide you with food and clothing. You are honest, you are industrious. Look upon me as your father."

After many years the father felt his end approaching, and he summoned his son and the officers of the king, and announced to them the secret that he had so long kept. The poor man was really his son, who in early days had wandered away from him; and now that he was conscious of his former debased condition, and was able to appreciate and retain vast wealth, he was determined to hand over to him his entire treasure. The poor man was astonished at this sudden change of fortune, and overjoyed at meeting his father once more.

The parables of Buddha are reported in the Lotus of the Perfect Law to be veiled from the ignorant by means of an enigmatic form of language.[1] The rich man of this parable, with his throne adorned by flowers and garlands of jewels, is announced to be Tathâgata, who dearly loves all his children, and has prepared for them vast spiritual treasures. But each son of Tathâgata has miserable inclinations. He prefers the dungheap to the pearl maṇi. To teach such a man, Tathâgata is obliged to employ inferior agents, the monk and the ascetic, and to wean him by degrees from the lower objects of desire. When he speaks himself, he is forced to veil much of his thought, as it would not be understood. His sons feel no joy on

[1] *Lotus*, p. 45.

hearing spiritual things. Little by little must their minds be trained and disciplined for higher truths.

PARABLE OF THE WOMAN AT THE WELL

Ânanda, a favourite disciple of Buddha, was once athirst, having travelled far. At a well he encountered a girl named Matanga, and asked her to give him some water to drink. But she, being a woman of low caste, was afraid of contaminating a holy Brâhmaṇa, and refused humbly.

"I ask not for caste, but for water!" said Ânanda. His condescension won the heart of the girl Matanga.

It happened that she had a mother cunning in love philtres and weird arts, and when this woman heard how much her daughter was in love, she threw her magic spells round the disciple and brought him to her cave. Helpless, he prayed to Buddha, who forthwith appeared and cast out the wicked demons.

But the girl Matanga was still in wretched plight. At last she determined to repair to Buddha himself and appeal to him.

The Great Physician, reading the poor girl's thought, questioned her gently:

"Supposing that you marry my disciple, can you follow him everywhere?"

"Everywhere!" said the girl.

"Could you wear his clothes, sleep under the same roof?" said Buddha, alluding to the nakedness and beggary of the "houseless one."

By slow degrees the girl began to take in his meaning, and at last she took refuge in the Three Great Pearls.[1]

[1] Burnouf, Introd. p. 138.

The Story of Vâsavadatta

At Maṭhurâ was a courtesan named Vâsavadatta. She fell violently in love with one of the actual disciples of Buddha named Upagupta, and sent her servant to him to declare her passion. Upagupta was young and of singular beauty. In a short time the servant returned with the following enigmatic reply:—

"The time has not yet arrived when the disciple Upagupta will pay a visit to the courtesan Vâsavadatta!"

Vâsavadatta was astonished at this reply. Her class at this time was a caste, a body organised, and indeed fostered, by the State, and she lived in great magnificence. She was the most beautiful woman in the king's dominions, and not accustomed to have her love rejected. When her first moments of petulance had passed, she reflected that the young man was poor. Again she sent her servant to Upagupta. "Tell him that Vâsavadatta desires love, not gold and pearls." By and by the servant returned with the enigmatic answer, "The time has not yet arrived when the disciple Upagupta will visit the courtesan Vâsavadatta!"

Some few months after this, Vâsavadatta had a love intrigue with the head of the artisans of Maṭhurâ, and whilst this was in progress a very wealthy merchant arrived at the city with five hundred horses that he desired to sell. Hearing of the beauty of Vâsavadatta, he contrived to see her, and also to fall in love with her. His pearls and suverṇas were too much for the giddy woman. She assassinated the head of the artisans and ordered his corpse to be flung on a dungheap. By and by his relations, alarmed at his disappearance, caused a search to be made, and the body was found.

Vâsavadatta was arrested and carried before the king, who gave orders that her ears, her nose, her hands, and her feet should at once be cut off by the common executioner and her body flung in a graveyard. Her maid still clung to her, for she had been a kind mistress. She tried to assuage her pain, and drove away the crows from her bleeding body.

Vâsavadatta now received a third message from Upagupta: "The time *has* arrived when the disciple Upagupta will pay a visit to the courtesan Vâsavadatta!" The poor woman, in whom an echo of the old passion still reverberated, hurriedly ordered her maid to collect and hide away under a cloth her severed feet and limbs, the poor remnants of her old beauty; and when the young man appeared she said with some petulance:

"Once this body was fragrant like the lotus, and I offered you my love. In those days I was covered with pearls and fine muslin. Now I am mangled and covered with filth and blood. My hands, my feet, my nose, my ears have been struck off by the common executioner!"

The young man with great gentleness comforted poor Vâsavadatta in her agony. "Sister, it is not for my pleasure and happiness that I now draw near." And he pointed out the "true nature" of the charms that she mourned. He showed her that they had proved torments and not joys, and if immodesty, and vanity, and greed, and the murderous instinct had been lopped away, she had sustained a gain and not a loss. He then told her of the Tathâgata that he had seen walking upon this very earth, a Tathâgata who specially loves the suffering.

His speech brought calm to the soul of Vâsavadatta. She died after having professed her faith in Buddha.[1]

She was carried by spirits to the penitential heavens of the Devaloca.

Parable of the Blazing Mansion

Once there was an old man, broken, decrepit, but very rich. He possessed much land and many gold pieces. Moreover, he possessed a large rambling mansion which also showed plain proofs of time's decay. Its rafters were worm-eaten; its pillars were rotten; its galleries were tumbling down; the thatch on its roof was dry and combustible. Inside this mansion were several hundreds of the old man's servants and retainers, so extensive was the collection of rambling old buildings.

Unfortunately this mansion possessed only one door.

The old man was also the father of many children —five, ten, twenty, let us say. One day there was a smell of burning, and he ran out by the solitary door. To his horror he saw the thatch in a mass of flame, the rotten old pillars were catching fire one by one, the rafters were blazing like tinder. Inside, his children, whom he loved most tenderly, were romping and amusing themselves with their toys.

The distracted father said to himself, "I will run

[1] Burnouf, Introd. pp. 131, 132.

in and save my children. I will seize them in my strong arms. I will bear them harmless through the falling rafters and the blazing beams!" Then the sad thought seized him that his children were romping and ignorant. "If I tell them that the house is on fire they will not understand me. If I try to seize them they will romp about and try to escape. Alas! not a moment is to be lost!"

Suddenly a bright thought flashed across the old man's mind. "My children are ignorant," he mentally said, "but they love toys and glittering playthings. I will promise them some playthings of unheard-of beauty. Then they will listen to me!"

So the old man shouted out with a loud voice, "Children, children, come out of the house and see these beautiful toys. Chariots with white oxen, all gold and tinsel. See these exquisite little antelopes! Whoever saw such goats as these! Children, children, come quickly or they will all be gone!"

Forth from the blazing ruin came the children in hot haste. The word "playthings" was almost the only word that they could understand. Then the fond father, in his great joy at seeing his offspring freed from peril, procured for them some of the most beautiful chariots ever seen. Each chariot had a canopy like a pagoda. It had tiny rails and balustrades and rows of jingling bells. It was formed of the seven precious substances. Chaplets of glittering pearls were hung aloft upon it; standards and wreaths of the most lovely flowers. Milk-white oxen drew these chariots. The children were astonished when they were placed inside.

The meaning of this parable is thus rendered in the

White Lotus of Dharma. The old man is Tathâgata, and his children the blind, suffering children of sin and passion. Tathâgata fondly loves them, and would save them from their unhappiness. The old rambling mansion, unsightly, rotten, perilous, is the domain of Kâma, the Domain of Appetite, the three great worlds of the visible kosmos. This old mansion is ablaze with the fire of mortal passions and hates and lusts. Tathâgata in his "immense compassion" would lead all his beloved children away from this great peril, but they do not understand his language. Their only thought is of tinsel toys and childish pastimes. If he speaks to them of the great inner quickening which makes man conquer human pain, they cannot understand him. If he talks to them of wondrous supernatural gifts accorded to mortals, they turn a deaf ear to him. The tinsel chariots provided for the children of Tathâgata are the "Greater" and "Lesser" Vehicles of the Buddhist teaching.

THE SERMON TO RÂHULA RESPECTING FALSEHOOD

Of the seven sacred books recognised in the days of Aśoka, one mentioned in the Bhabra edict has lately come to light; and this has been found not in the vaunted ancient canon of Ceylon, but in China. I give this short work *in extenso* as translated by the invaluable Professor Beal.[1]

"In days of old, before Râhula had attained to supreme wisdom, his natural disposition being somewhat low and disorderly, his words were not always marked by love of truth. On one occasion Buddha

[1] *Dhammapada*, p. 142.

had ordered him to go to the Kien-tai [Ghanda or Ghanta?] Vihâra, and there remain guarding his mouth [tongue] and governing his thoughts, at the same time diligently studying [or observing] the rules of conduct laid down in the scriptures. Râhula, having heard the command, made his obeisance and went. For ninety days he remained in deep shame and penitence. At length Buddha repaired to the place and showed himself. On seeing him, Râhula was filled with joy, and reverently bowed down and worshipped him. After this, Buddha having taken the seat provided for him, he desired Râhula to fill a water-basin with water and bring it to him and wash his feet. Having done so, and the washing being over, Buddha asked Râhula if the water so used was now fit for any purpose of domestic use [drinking, etc.]; and on Râhula replying in the negative because the water was defiled with dust and dirt, Buddha added, 'And such is your case; for although you are my son and the grandchild of the king, although you have voluntarily given up everything to become a Shaman, nevertheless you are unable to guard your tongue from untruth and the defilement of loose conversation, and so you are like this defiled water—useful for no further purpose.' And again he asked him, after the water had been thrown away, whether the vessel was now fit for holding water to drink; to which Râhula replied, 'No, for the vessel is still defiled, and is known as an unclean thing, and therefore not used for any purpose such as that indicated.' To which Buddha again replied, 'And such is your case. By not guarding your tongue, etc., you are known and recognised as unfit for any high purpose, although you profess to be a Shaman.' And then once more lifting the empty basin on to his foot, and whirling it round and round, he asked Râhula if he were not afraid lest it should fall and be broken; to which Râhula replied that he had no such fear, for the vessel was but a cheap and common one, and therefore its loss would be a matter of small moment. 'And such is your case,' again said Buddha; 'for though you are a Shaman, yet, being unable to guard your mouth or your tongue, you are destined, as a small and insignificant thing, to be whirled in the endless eddies of transmigration, an object of contempt to all the wise.' Râhula being filled with shame, Buddha addressed him once more. 'Listen, and I will speak to you a parable. There was in old time the king of a certain country, who had a large and very powerful elephant, able to overpower by its own strength five hundred smaller elephants. This king, being about to go to war with some rebellious dependency, brought forth the iron armour belonging to the elephant, and directed the master of the animal to put it on him, to wit, two sharp-pointed swords on his tusks, two iron hooks [scythes] on his ears, a crooked spear on each foot, an iron club [or ball] attached to his tail, and to accompany him were appointed nine soldiers as escort. Then the elephant-master rejoiced to see the creature thus equipped, and trained him above all things to keep his trunk well coiled up, knowing that an arrow piercing *that* in the midst must be fatal. But lo! in the middle of the battle the elephant, uncoiling his trunk, sought to seize a sword with it. On which the master was affrighted, and, in consultation with the king and his ministers, it was agreed that he should no more be brought into the battlefield.' In continuation Buddha said: 'Râhula! if men, committing the nine faults, only guard their tongue as this elephant was trained to guard his trunk, all would be well. Let them guard against the arrow that strikes in the middle! let them keep their mouth, lest they die, and fall into the misery of future births in the three evil paths!' And then he added these stanzas:—

"'I am like the fighting elephant without any fear of the middle arrow [the arrow wounding the middle part]. By sincerity and truth I escape the unprincipled man [lawless man]. Like the elephant, well subdued and quiet, who permits the king to mount on his trunk [offers his trunk for the king to ascend], thus tamed is the reverend man; he also endures truthfully and in faith.'

"Râhula, hearing these words, was filled with sorrow for his careless disregard of his words, and gave himself up to renewed exertion, and so became a Rahat."

Externals

Against Buddha's teaching two main objections have been urged:

1. That his Bodhi, viewed from a spiritual point of view, is mere selfishness. The individual isolates himself from his race for his own advantage.

2. The monkish system that he spread abroad has, in point of fact, produced many grave evils—idleness, immorality, depravity, etc. — and is, in fact, pure

pessimism. One answer meets both objections, that is, as far as they are unjust.

The problem before a reformer in Buddha's day was essentially practical. To enfranchise the world, what possible apparatus was available? The oratory of the uninspired demagogue would not have been listened to by the masses, and would have been quickly silenced by the dominant caste. Books, printing presses, even the letters of the alphabet were unavailable; and the victories of material force in Buddha's view meant merely the firmer riveting of chains. So Buddha, himself a king, in commencing his conflict, handed over an army of soldiers and an army of priests to his antagonists, determined that the victory should be a purely moral one. One weapon alone was within reach — the tree of the Ṛishi. Under that tree God spake. Such was the belief of the people, based on the teaching of the Vedic hymns, as recited at every sacrifice. With Buddha the Bodhi meant not selfishness, but the complete conquest of self; and the initiation of the Ṛishi under his tree was merely a means to an end. Instead of being sloth, that end was boundless activity in contributing to the happiness of others. His blameless soldiers, having given up wife and wealth, were ordered to march from tree to tree, never resting for two nights under the same one. No halt was to be allowed but the grave as long as a king oppressed his subjects, a priest tortured animals, or as long as spiritual ignorance tortured priests and kings.

Viewed from the historical side, the following originalities may be accredited to Buddhism:—

1. Enforced vegetarianism for the whole nation.

2. Enforced national abstinence from wine.

3. Abolition of slavery.

4. The introduction of the principle of forgiveness of injuries in opposition to the national *lex talionis.*

5. Uncompromising antagonism to all national religious rites that were opposed to the gnosis or spiritual development of the individual.

6. Beggary, continence, and asceticism for the religious teachers.

These are the six originalities of the Buddhist movement, as viewed from the outside.

Up to the age of eighty, the indefatigable old man carried on his preachings, chiefly in modern Behar (a corruption of Vihâra, the old word for monastery). The ancient books scarcely help us here, owing to Eastern exaggerations and Eastern romance. Kings everywhere bow to him humbly, and converts come in, not by thousands but by tens of thousands. From Patna he marches to Râjâgṛiha, and from Râjâgṛiha to Kapilavastu, founding monasteries everywhere. On this point we have more to say by and by.

DEATH OF BUDDHA

Some eighty miles due east of Buddha's birthplace, Kapilavastu, now stands a modest village called Mâthâ Kuär (the "Dead Prince"). At the date of the pilgrimage of Hwen Thsang there was a reason for this. Under a splendid temple-canopy reposed in marble a "Dead Prince," and this circumstance is still remembered by the natives. The ruins of this temple can still be traced. Exactly four hundred and seventy years before Christ the spot was a jaṅgal of Śâla-trees, and beneath the shade of two of these lay calm and rigid the gentle teacher whom Indians call the "Best Friend of all the World." Buddha was journeying from Râjâgṛiha when he reached this resting-place. Its name was Kuśinagara. At Beluva, near Vaiśâlî, he was attacked with a severe illness. Violent pains seized him. He was very nearly dying. Ânanda was disconsolate, but Buddha comforted him.

"What need hath the body of my followers of me now, Ânanda? I have declared the doctrine, and I have made no distinction between within and without. He who says, 'I will rule over the Sañgha!' or, 'Let the Sañgha be subjected to me!' he, Ânanda, might declare his will in the Church. The Tathâgata, however, does not say, 'I will rule over the Church.' . . . I am now frail, Ânanda; I am aged, I am an old man who has finished his pilgrimage and reached old age. Eighty years old am I.

"Be to yourselves, Ânanda, your own light, your own refuge. Seek no other refuge. Let Dharma be your light and refuge. Seek no other refuge. . . . Whosoever now, Ânanda, or after my departure, shall be his own light, his own refuge, and shall seek no other refuge, will henceforth be my true disciple and walk in the right path."

Buddha journeyed on until he reached a place called Pâvâ. There he was attacked with a grievous sickness. Weary, the old pilgrim reached a stream, the Kakutthâ (the modern Badhi, according to General Cunningham). Buddha bathed and sipped some of the water; carts were passing and they thickened it with mud. A little farther on, by the side of the river Háranyavatî (Chota Gandak), was a grove of Śâla-trees. Between two of these blossoming trees was the Nirvâṇa that the sick and weary pilgrim was sighing for.

Under these two famous trees, with his head lying towards the north, the old man was laid. "Weep not, sorrow not, Ânanda," he said. "From all that man loves and enjoys he must tear himself.

"My existence is ripening to its close. The end of my life is near. I go hence. Ye remain behind. The place of refuge is ready for me."[1]

Before expiring, the teacher entered into the extasia of Samâdhi; and mighty thunders and earth-rockings announced the passing away of a great Chakravartin. Buddha's last words were:

"Hearken, O disciples, I charge you. All that comes into being passes. Seek your salvation without weariness."

[1] Oldenberg, *Buddha*, p. 199.

CHAPTER VI

AFTER BUDDHA'S DEATH

I HAVE found, after much investigation, and I hope to convince the reader, that the progress and evolution of Buddhism can best be made intelligible by dividing its advance into four distinct periods.

1. March of the formidable *Parivrâjikas* across India. Their monasteries were trees; their temples were forests; their monks' cowls, tree-bark; their gospel, the inner light.

2. Conversion of King Aśoka, whose rule over India was more extensive than that of any Mogul. A more official and definite religion was required for this large empire. Date of King Aśoka, B.C. 257.

3. Rise of the Gospel of Flat Contradiction and its corollary, the worship of the coming and dethronement of the past Buddha, two expedients considered necessary in introducing the *Śunyavâdi's* creed, namely, that men and gods, even the highest, come from Nothingness or *Śunya*, and after a sickly dream of unreal worlds return to *Śunya*.

4. Recoil, and rise of the *Aiswarikas*, who, finding Buddha's pedestal vacant, set up the "Eternal Life Buddha" (*Amitâyas* or *Amitâbha*), with his eternal paradise (*Sukhâvatî*).

When Buddhism came to Europe it was spread

by a sort of freemasonry. In an early work I suggested that perhaps in India a similar expedient may have been at starting adopted. For this I was taken to task in the *Indian Antiquary* for my "crass ignorance." The critic pointed triumphantly to the abundant chronicles of the southern Buddhists,—but are they quite reliable? Let us consider the narrative of the early Buddhist movement as given by Professor Rhys Davids in his *Birth Stories.*

Buddha, as we know, first preached the law in a deer forest, about four miles to the north of the holy city of Benares. The spot is called Sârnâth (Sâruggânâtha, the "Lord of Deer") to this day. Aśoka built a splendid temple in this wilderness. The dome is ninety-three feet in diameter, and its imposing mass still dominates the plain. Pilgrims from China have visited it; and pilgrims from all countries in the world go to it still. It is called Dhamek, a corruption for the Temple of Dharma. Now, the Cingalese historian, evidently writing long after this temple of Dharma had become famous, makes Buddha put up in a fine temple and vihâra in a "suburb of Benares"[1] during the first rainy season after his conversion.

Benares was already the most holy city of the Hindoos, and yet it is recorded that Buddha preached openly against the Brahmin religion, and made sixty-one converts.

He then proceeded to the powerful Brahmin kingdom of Magadha, and arrived at the capital, Râjâgṛiha, attended by over a thousand followers. The king at once became a convert, with a large proportion of his

[1] *Buddhist Birth Stories*, p. 91.

subjects; and handed over to Buddha the grove in which the celebrated Veṇuvana monastery was afterwards situated. The Cingalese writer does not take the trouble to say a word about the building of it, being evidently under an impression that it was already there. Five months after Buddha had attained the Bodhi, he started off to Kapilavastu, a distance of sixty leagues, to see his father. He was accompanied by twenty thousand, yellow-robed, shaven Bhikshus; and he marched along the highroads of the various Brahmin kingdoms that were on his road without any molestation. At Kapilavastu he found another fine vihâra ready for him; and the bulk of the nation and the king became converts to his religion. He returned shortly to Râjâgṛiha to find a convenient merchant ready at once to hand over to him the rich vihâra, or monastery, of Jetavana at Śrâvastî (Sahet Mahet). Buddha went at once to the spot; and this time the chronicler allows a vihâra to be built, a *new* one, he again fancying apparently that one was there. There was "a pleasant room for the sage," separate apartments for "eighty elders," and "other residences with single and double walls, and long halls and open roofs ornamented with ducks and quails; and ponds also he made, and terraces to walk on by day and by night."[1]

When Buddha arrived at Śrâvastî this convent was dedicated to him by the merchant, who went through a formula well known in the ancient inscriptions of Ceylon. He poured water out of a bowl, and made over the land to the monks. Then a gorgeous festival took place, which lasted nine months.

[1] *Buddhist Birth Stories*, p. 130.

Exactly five hundred and forty millions of gold pieces were expended on this feast and on the convent; so that we may presume, I suppose, that most of the inhabitants of the powerful Brahmin kingdom of Śrâvastî had become converts. Thus, in less than a year, Buddha had practically converted the Brahmin kingdoms that stretch from Śrâvastî (Sahet Mahet) to Gayâ.

In a word, his creed had already won what is called the Holy Land of the Buddhists.

Is all this true? Even by lopping off Eastern exaggerations and accretions, can we reduce it in any way to a plausible story? If the Buddhism set forth by Dr. Rhys Davids, or even by M. Barthélemy St. Hilaire, be the real Buddhism that was preached by Buddha, I say that the task is impossible. If in the holiest city of the Hindoos, Buddha had proclaimed that there was no God, and in a complete and categorical manner had announced that man had no soul, nor anything of any sort that existed after death, the cruel laws of the Brahmins against heresy would have been put in force against him. Dr. Rhys Davids contends that it is proved by the Upanishads that "absolute freedom of thought" existed in ancient India.[1] But the Upanishads were secret,—he forgets that. They were whispered to pupils who had passed through a severe probation. Megasthenes, the Greek ambassador to Patna, bears witness to this.[2]

To assail a Brahmin, his privileges and class interests was the one sin in those days for which there was no forgiveness. We see this from the laws of Manu. Buddha, in every sermon, assailed these root and branch. He denounced the caste system, the bloody

[1] *Hibbert Lectures*, p. 26. [2] Cory, *Ancient Fragments*, p. 225.

sacrifice, the use of wine in the Soma sacrifice, the lucrative pilgrimages. In a word, the principal sources of priestly revenue and ascendency were freely assailed.

Another great difficulty about the early years of Buddha's ministry is this monastery (vihâra) question. It is plain that Dr. Rhys Davids' biography is the work either of a pious knave giving the sanction of Buddha to large donations for convents, processions, etc., or of a pious fool too dull to draw any picture except that of the late and corrupt Buddhism that was under his nose. The real question is, Did the earliest disciples dwell in any vihâra at all?

From the North we get an important set of Buddhist rules — the "Twelve Observances." The "Mob of Beggars," as Buddha called his followers, are expressly forbidden to have any covering over them except a tree. Their "one seat" is to be mother earth. Their clothes are to be rags from the dustheap, the dung-heap, the graveyard. The tree that covers the beggar must be, if possible, in a graveyard. He is to be called Durkhrodpa ("He who lives in a graveyard"). He is not allowed to sleep twice under the same tree.[1]

These rules, if genuine, put the Cingalese chronicles out of court. Let us consider the vihâra as an apparatus of propagandism. Could it have conquered India? Could it have conquered Asia?

Buddha in person, in Dr. Rhys Davids' translation, tells us the functions of vihâras:

> "Cold they ward off, and heat;
> So also beasts of prey
> And creeping things and gnats,
> And rains in the cold season;

[1] Burnouf, Introd. pp. 269, 274.

And when the dreaded heat and winds
Arise they ward them off.
To give to monks a dwelling-place
Wherein in safety and in peace
To think till mysteries grow clear,
The Buddha calls a worthy deed.
Let, therefore, a wise man,
Regarding his own weal,
Have pleasant monasteries built,
And lodge there learned men.
Let him with cheerful mien
Give food to them and drink,
And clothes and dwelling-places
To the upright in mind.
Then shall they preach to him the truth."[1]

If this translation of Dr. Rhys Davids gives us, as it professes to do, the truest and most authentic account available of a vihâra in the first year of Buddha's preaching, we gather that the chief objects of a vihâra were:

1. To afford shelter, clothes, food, and comfort to a recluse whilst he developed his individual spiritualism.

2. To keep off from the monks the floods of the rainy season, the great heats of the hot season, the fiery blasts of the season of the hot winds, and the cold of winter. Moreover, the vihâra was to be "pleasant."

Now, if the monk resided in his vihâra in the hot season, and during the rains and hot winds and in the cold season, it is difficult to see when he acted as missionary, for a monk in a monastery is called the silent one (*Muni*). In his walks abroad he may present his begging-bowl, but must not speak. A regulation

[1] *Birth Stories*, p. 132.

exists that the monk should devote himself to silent meditation during the rainy season (*Varshâ*);[1] but this rule must have been issued long subsequent to the issue of the "Twelve Observances," as it stultifies them.

Vihâra propagandism may be good for a country which is already Buddhist; but I fail to see how it could make a country of Buddhists. And yet some very active propagandism must have leavened India from one end to the other before Aśoka made Buddhism the official creed. The Holy Land of the Buddhists—and it is to that that Buddha's own preaching was almost completely confined—was an insignificant portion of Aśoka's vast dominions. He tells us that Gândhâra (Peshawur), to the north, and Chola and Pândiya, the extreme southern provinces of Hindostan, had become converted. On the extreme west, at Girnâr, near the Gulf of Cutch, a rock inscription was cut. On the eastern coast, at Ganjam, were the Dhauli and Jaugada inscriptions. To Ceylon, and to Bactria, and to Egypt the Buddhist missionaries, as he announces, had also gone.

Bishop Bigandet's history, the Burmese scripture, gives a different colouring to these early days. It makes Buddha go not to a suburb of Benares, where there was a vihâra, but to Mṛigadava, the "deer forest," near Benares. When he leaves Benares he makes his way towards the "desert of Uravilva." It is under a tree in a forest that he is found by the profligate young men whom he converts on his journey. At Gayâ it is on a mountain that he preaches. When

[1] Hwen Thsang, *Mémoires*, vol. i. p. 64.

he nears Râjâgṛiha he repairs to a "palm grove." The king presents to him, not the vihâra, but the "Garden of Bamboos" (Veṇuvana). When he visits Kapilavastu he goes to the "Grove of Banyan-Trees," and so on.

Buddha's instructions also to his disciples are more in harmony with the account given of early Buddhism in the "Twelve Observances" than in the Cingalese version.

"A great duty is yours—to work for the happiness of men and spirits. Let us separate and go each in a different direction, no two following the same road. Go and preach Dharma."

At the risk of getting a subtle thinker like Dr. Oldenberg also charged with "crass ignorance" by the critic of the *Indian Antiquary*, I must mention that he also considers that there is little in this portion of Buddha's life that deserves even the name of "tradition," but "merely collections of countless real or feigned addresses, dialogues, and sayings of Buddha." The doctor affirms, also, that from the Cingalese books, the "tarrying of ascetics under trees might be multiplied *ad libitum*." Where else, he says, could they sit in Buddha's time? The following citation he gives from the Cûlahatthi pado pama sutta:—

"He dwells in a lonely spot, in a grove, at the foot of a tree, on a mountain, in a cave, in a mountain grotto, in a burialplace, in the wilderness, under an open sky, on a heap of straw." That was plainly early Buddhism.

The Russian Orientalist, Wassiljew, may here be cited. He gives a fact from a Chinese translation of a history, attributed to Daranatha, the grandson of Aśoka. Daranatha announces that a disciple of Ânanda reached Cashmir. This means, of course, covert propagandism at a very early date.

In the British Museum are the marbles of the Amarâvatî Tope. I see strangers, with puzzled look, stop before certain tablets that represent marble worshippers crouching before a small throne or table placed before a marble tree. On the altar are often two footprints. More learned inquirers have been equally puzzled. But the recent exhumation of the remains of the Stûpa of Bharhut (B.C. 250) has placed the meaning of these emblems beyond the region of controversy. Similar designs have been there discovered, and they are furnished with explanations incised in the Pâli character. One, it is said, is the throne and tree of Kaśyapa, another the throne and tree of Kanaka Muni, and so on through the list of the Seven Great Buddhas. Every Great Buddha has his tree and his worship. And here I must mention a curious piece of Chinese-puzzle adjustment, which shows how closely the ritual fits the ancient temple, and the temple the ritual. In vol. xvi. of the *Asiatic Researches*, Professor Wilson gives a ritual from Nepâl, called the Praise of the Seven Buddhas (p. 453). Each Buddha is "adored" in a separate paragraph, and it is announced that he found emancipation under a special tree. Comparing the list of these trees with that of the Bharhut Stûpa, as given by General Cunningham,[1] we find that five of the trees exactly correspond. The sixth, that of Visvabhû, is obliterated. Śâkya Muni's tree in one list is the aśvattha, and in

[1] *Stûpa of Bharhut*, p. 46.

the other the pippala — synonyms for the *Ficus religiosa.* This seems to give great antiquity to the litany.

I will copy down one or two of these addresses:

"I adore Jinendra, the consuming fire of sorrow, the treasure of holy knowledge whom all revere, who bore the name of Vipasvi, who was born in the race of mighty monarchs in the city of Bandumati, who was for eighty thousand years the preceptor of gods and men; and by whom, endowed with the ten kinds of power, the degree of Jinendra was obtained at the foot of a pâṭala-tree."

This is the praise of Śâkya Muni:

"I adore Śâkya Simha the Buddha, the kinsman of the sun, worshipped by men and gods, who was born at the splendid city Kapilapura, of the family of the chief of the Śâkya kings, the life of which best friend to all the world lasted one hundred years. Having speedily subdued desire, unbounded wisdom was acquired by him at the foot of the aśvattha-tree."[1]

We now come to a valuable piece of testimony, that of a Greek visiting India. Seleucus Nicator sent an ambassador, named Megasthenes, to King Chandragupta (B.C. 302 – 298). He visited that monarch at his capital, Palibothra, or Patna. His account of the India of that day is unfortunately lost; but through Diodorus Siculus, Strabo, Arrian, and Clement of Alexandria, some valuable fragments have come down to us. Patna, it must be remembered, was in the very heart of the Buddhist Holy Land. Clement of Alexandria cites a passage from

[1] *Asiatic Researches,* xvi. p. 454.

Megasthenes *On Indian Affairs.* On the same page he thus describes the Indian "philosophers":—

"Of these there are two classes, some of them called Sarmanæ and others Brahmins. And those of the Sarmanæ who are called Hylobii neither inhabit cities nor have roofs over them, but are clothed in the bark of trees, feed on nuts, and drink water in their hands. Like those called Encratites in the present day, they know not marriage nor begetting of children. Some, too, of the Indians obey the precepts of Buddha, whom, on account of his extraordinary sanctity, they have raised to divine honours."

The importance of this passage is this, that from Strabo we get the description given by Megasthenes of the Indian philosophers, and it is made certain that the earlier part of this passage is from the same source.

Strabo describes the Brahmins and the "Germanes," also called, he says, "Hylobii." He gives the same details as Clement of Alexandria about their feeding on wild fruits and wearing the bark of trees. He, too, draws a distinction between the Germanes and the Brahmins on the subject of continency, the Brahmins being polygamists.

From this it seems certain that Clement of Alexandria was writing with the original work of Megasthenes before him. We may therefore conclude that this passage about Buddha, sandwiched as it is between two genuine citations, was also in Megasthenes. Strabo has handed down to us another statement of Megasthenes about the Hylobii:

"By their means the kings serve and worship the Deity."

There can be no doubt that the Sarmanes (Śramaṇas) and Brahmins of Megasthenes were the Brahmins and the Buddhists. To the first, according to Megasthenes, were confided sacrifices and ceremonies, for the dead as well as the living. They were a caste apart, and none outside this caste could perform their duties. The gods would not accept the sacrifices of such an interloper. Their ideas on life and death were very similar to those of Plato and the Greeks. The Brahmins ate flesh and had many wives. Every new year there was a great synod of them. They dwelt in groves near the great cities, on "couches of leaves and skins."

The Hylobii, on the other hand, insisted on absolute continence, and strict vegetarianism and water-drinking. Clitarchus gives us an additional fact. Megasthenes, we learn from him, has also recorded that the Hylobii "derided the Brahmins."

The First Convocation

Buddha died miserably under a tree, but, according to Buddhaghosa, there were near Râjâgṛiha at the moment of his death eighteen great monasteries "filled with rubbish." The monks determined to repair these great monasteries, and they went to the King of Râjâgṛiha and said to him: "Mahârâja, we propose to hold a great convocation on religion and discipline. On the Webhara Mountain is a cave called Sattapanni. Be graciously pleased to prepare that cave for us!"

The king at once gave orders that a mighty cave-temple should be scooped out of the rock. A "hall," with "pillars" and "walls," was executed as if by the hand of Viśvakarma, the architect of heaven. "Flights of steps, embellished with representations of festoons of flowers and of flower-creepers, rivalling the splendour of the decorations of his palace, and imitating the magnificence of the mansions of the devas," were constructed. Five hundred carpeted seats were prepared for the monks, and a pulpit for the principal. A preaching desk, "for the sanctified Buddha himself," in the centre of the hall facing the east, was erected, and an ivory fan placed upon it. This incident shows, I think, that the early sermon-monger was supposed to get his inspiration direct from the dead Tathâgata.

In two months this great cave-temple was completed; and the monks were summoned. A difficulty arose about Ânanda, who had not acquired the miraculous powers that stamp the adept in the knowledge of Prajñâ Pâramitâ, the wisdom of the unseen world. Thus, as first constituted, the convocation consisted of 499 members, and a vacant carpet was spread for Ânanda. During the night he meditated on the Kâyagastâ Satiyâ, and in the morning these powers came; and in proof he reached his seat through the medium of the floor of the temple.

Mahâ Kaśyapa was the chief Thêrô, and he opened the proceedings by requesting Upali to detail Buddha's injunctions on discipline. Upali before answering sat in the pulpit of Buddha, and held the mystic ivory fan. Three hundred and four Sikkhapadini on form and rites were wearily gone through. After Upali detailed each section the monks at once chanted it forth. When Upali took the mystic fan in his hand the mighty earth quaked. As the narrative announces that this was done to give the assembly a greeting similar to the one that Buddha used to give his Arhats, I think the idea plainly was that, instead of being annihilated, the great teacher was present, obsessing Upali in his chair. After Upali had revealed all that he recollected from Buddha's lips on the subject of discipline, Ânanda stepped into the "pulpit of the sanctified Buddha himself," and detailed all the utterances that he could call to mind about Dharma. The Northern account gives to Ânanda the Sûtras, and to Kaśyapa the department of Prajñâ Pâramitâ, or Dharma. The convocation sat for seven months. Earthquakes and other miracles greeted its finish.

Now it seems to me we are here in the presence of a piece of pure history. The details of the great cave-temple with its mats, pulpits, ivory fan, chanting monks, etc., are too lifelike to be absolute invention. The incident of the eighteen tumbledown vihâras filled with rubbish but hastily got ready is not the sort of incident that would have suggested itself to a Cingalese writer of fiction. The Mahâwanso, describing the great banquets during Aśoka's inauguration, announces that elks, wild hogs, and winged game came to the king's kitchen of their own accord, and then expired; that parrots daily brought nine hundred thousand loads of hill paddy, and mice husking that hill paddy converted it into rice. The fine fancy of a Cingalese historian, if left to itself, would have gone off into similar flights.

But if the convocation described is a *bonâ fide* convocation, it cannot be the first convocation of the Cingalese records; nor yet the second, nor even the third. The cave, which is thought to be the Sattapanni cave (though its identity is questioned by Mr. Fergusson), is, according to that authority, a natural cave "slightly improved by art."[1] In Aśoka's day the cave-temple was a small cave without sculpture, and with merely a polished roof. Even in Kaniśka's day there was no cave-temple of the gorgeous pattern here described. This gives a very modern date to the narrative. It gives us, I think, without any doubt, some details of Kaniśka's convocation. Observe that the number of monks in Kaniśka's convocation, and the number of monks in the first convocation as recorded by Buddhaghosa, are in each case exactly 499. In each case, also, this is made up to 500 by a monk performing a miracle.

It must be remembered that if, in the third or fourth century of our era, a writer in Ceylon were drawing up a history of the convocations, the details of the last one would naturally be the most prominent in his mind. He would see the panorama of history reversed. The last convocation would be clear, the second and first dim and shadowy. I must point out, too, that the incident of the chanting monks could not have taken place, as described in the Ceylon books. It would be quite impossible to get 500 monks to learn by heart a voluminous canon, four times as long as our Bible, in the time given. Two contradictory narratives have been made use of—a story similar to the Northern story, which announced

[1] *Indian Architecture*, p. 108.

that three disciples collected the scanty scraps of the remembered precepts of Buddha three months after his death, and a narrative of Kaniśka's convocation, which would have had the incident of the chanting monks. At that period they *could* have sung out all the canonical books, as they knew them by heart.

But the evidence that Buddhaghosa's account of the first convocation has been largely made up from details of Kaniśka's convocation is by no means exhausted. The chief individual work discussed was the Brahmajâla Sûtra. Mahâ Kaśyapa, the president, asked Ânanda which Sûtra should be first considered.

"Lord, the Brahmajâla Sûtra," said Ânanda.

"Let us then rehearse first that Sûtra," said the president, "which triumphed over the various heretical faiths sustained by hypocrisy and fraud, which unravelled the doctrinal issue of the sixty-two heterodox sects, and shook the earth together with its ten thousand component parts." When Ânanda had explained all about this Sûtra, the earth rocked. "All the thirteen Sûtras," says the narrative, "were then rehearsed in the prescribed forms."

This little passage lets the cat quite out of the bag. The Brahmajâla Sûtra is the Bible of Pyrrho-Buddhism. M. de Rémusat,[1] in his translation of Fa Hian's *Voyages*, announces that it is called a Mahâyâna tractate by Hoa Yen, the leading Chinese authority on the Great Vehicle literature. Mr. Bunyiu Nanjio, the accomplished Japanese scholar recently employed at the India Office to draw up a catalogue of the

[1] *Pilgrimage of Fa Hian*, p. 108, note.

Buddhist scriptures, also pronounces it to belong to the literature of the Mahâyâna movement. This might have thrown some suspicion in the minds of those who were making it the brief for their great impeachment of Buddha.

The facts here stated, if placed in two parallel columns, will make more convincing still our conclusion that the story of the first convocation is a dishonest fiction invented to give the authority of age to the Brahmâjâla Sûtra.

Convocation of Râjâgriha, B.C. 470.	*Convocation of King Kaniška,* A.D. 16.
Had 499 members and a vacant seat.	Had 499 members and a vacant seat.
Excluded monk performs a silly miracle.	Excluded monk performs a silly miracle.
He is admitted and made chief instructor of the Assembly.	He is admitted and made chief instructor of the Assembly.
Council triumphs over "sixty-two heretical sects."	Council triumphs over numberless heretics.
Approves of Pyrrho-Buddhism as set forth in the Brahmâjâla Sûtra.	Called together, especially to establish Pyrrho-Buddhism.

THE SECOND CONVOCATION

Of this convocation we need not say much. There is nothing about it in the Northern records, and Mr. Turnour, in vol. vi. of the *Journal of the Bengal Asiatic Society*, gives good reasons for believing that its record is a simple fiction invented by Buddhaghosa. It is said to have occurred at Vaišâlî one hundred years after the first (that is, B.C. 370), or about seventy years before Megasthenes visited Patna, a spot about twenty miles from Vaiśâlî. The chief point debated was whether monks living in sumptuous monasteries might or might not have fringes to their couches. The monks in those regions at the date of Megasthenes had couches of mother earth fringed only with thistles.

CHAPTER VII

KING AŚOKA

In Buddha Gayâ, in the year B.C. 520, Buddha sat under a *pippala* tree dreaming of a *Dharma Râj*. We have all our visions at times of this *Dharma Râj*, a bright kingdom of Dreamland where wrong is righted; but who, like Buddha, sees his dream made concrete?

Buddha sat under the renowned *Ficus religiosa*, B.C. 520. Two hundred and fifty years after this appeared King Aśoka and the *Dharma Râj*.

Aśoka, at the age of twenty-four, succeeded to the throne of Patna. His brothers raised troops, and sought to upset him. After a sharp struggle he overcame them, and treated them with the usual mercy of Asiatics towards brothers near the throne. He was the grandson of Sandrocottus, who was placed on the throne by Brahmin intrigue. Aśoka was at first a pious Brahmin, and 50,000 Brahmins were fed by him daily. Also he was a capable soldier, for he conquered more Indian territory than Clive, Lake, Wellington, and Napier, if they were to sum up the area of their united conquests.

But after his consecration he had several conversations with a Buddhist monk named Nigrauda. Much interested in Buddha, he received eagerly the details of his life and teaching. Soon the king was converted, and he made Buddhism the State religion.

Shortly before this, according to the calculations of Sir Alexander Cunningham and Professor Max Müller, India received the letters of the alphabet. The gift was happily timed, because the first use made of it was to scratch ideas on rocks and stones. In the year B.C. 251, King Aśoka incised his earliest rock edict. He soon issued a great many more. Some idea of the extent of his rule and the spread of Buddhism may be gained from the fact that on the extreme west of India he cut a rock inscription at Girnâr on the Gulf of Cutch. On the east coast, at Ganjam, were the Dhauli and Jaugada edicts; and Gândhâra, or Peshawur, was reached in the north; and Chola and Pândiya, the extreme southern provinces of India, as I have said before.

I have said that it was a fortunate circumstance that the rude expedient was adopted of cutting the edicts on stone, because innovators cannot treat stone edicts like manuscripts on plantain leaves; and we get at once an opportunity of finding out at least what Buddha's disciples thought about God, spirit, and man's future.

King Aśoka's Ideas about God

"Much longing after the things [of this life] is a disobedience, I again declare; not less so is the laborious ambition of dominion by a prince who would be a propitiator of Heaven. Confess and believe in God [Îśâna], who is the worthy object of obedience. For equal to this [belief], I declare unto you, ye shall not find such a means of propitiating Heaven. Oh, strive ye to obtain this inestimable treasure."[1]

"Thus spake King Devânampiya Piyadasi: The present moment and the past have departed under the same ardent hopes. How by the conversion of the royal born may religion be increased? Through the conversion of the lowly born if religion thus increaseth, by how much [more] through the conviction of the high born and their conversion shall religion increase? Among whomsoever the name of God resteth, verily this is religion."

"Thus spake Devânampiya Piyadasi: Wherefore from this very hour I have caused religious discourses to be preached. I have appointed religious observances that mankind, having listened thereto, shall be brought to follow in the right path, and give glory to God."[2]

"It is well known, sirs, to what lengths have gone my respect for and faith in Buddha, Dharma, Sañgha."[3]

"Whatever words have been spoken by the divine Buddha, they have all been well said."[4]

"And he who acts in conformity with this edict shall be united with Sugato."[5]

"The white elephant, whose name is The Bringer of Happiness to the Whole World."[6]

Îśâna is the name that has been selected by the Sanskrit scholars employed recently in translating "God save the Queen." Buddha, Dharma, and Sañgha make up the Buddhist Trinity, which is precisely

[1] First Separate Edict, Dhauli, Prinsep.
[2] Edict No. VII., Prinsep. [3] Second Bairât Rock, Burnouf.
[4] Second Bairât Rock, Wilson. [5] Delhi Pillar, Prinsep.
[6] Final Sentence of the Rock Edicts, Kern.

similar to that of Philo and the Gnostics. Buddha is spirit; Dharma, matter; Sañgha, ideal humanity, the Christ. They figure together as three beings in the sculptures of Buddha Gayâ, one of Aśoka's temples. Later on they got also to mean Buddha, his law and his monks.

Aśoka on a Future Life

"On the many beings over whom I rule I confer happiness in this world; in the next they may obtain Swarga [paradise]." [1]

"This is good. With these means let a man seek Swarga. This is to be done. By these means it is to be done, as by them Swarga [paradise] is to be gained." [2]

"I pray with every variety of prayer for those who differ with me in creed, that they, following after my example, may with me attain unto eternal salvation." [3]

"And whoso doeth this is blessed of the inhabitants of this world; and in the next world endless moral merit resulteth from such religious charity." [4]

"Unto no one can be repentance and peace of mind until he hath obtained supreme knowledge, perfect faith, which surmounteth all obstacles, and perpetual assent." [5]

"In the tenth year of his anointment, the beloved King Piyadasi obtained the Sambodhi, or complete knowledge." [6]

"All the heroism that Piyadasi, the beloved of the gods, has exhibited is in view of another life. Earthly glory brings little profit, but, on the contrary, produces

[1] Edict VI., Wilson.
[2] Edict IX., Wilson.
[3] Delhi Pillar, Edict VI., Prinsep.
[4] Edict XI., Prinsep.
[5] Rock Edict, No. VII., Prinsep.
[6] Rock Edict, No. VII., Burnouf.

a loss of virtue. To toil for heaven is difficult to peasant and to prince, unless by a supreme effort he gives up all."[1]

"May they [my loving subjects] obtain happiness in this world and in the next."[2]

"The beloved of the gods speaketh thus: It is more than thirty-two years and a half that I am a hearer of the law, and I did not exert myself strenuously; but it is a year or more that I have entered the community of ascetics, and that I have exerted myself strenuously. Those gods who during this time were considered to be true gods in Jambudvîpa have now been abjured. . . . A small man who exerts himself somewhat can gain for himself great heavenly bliss, and for this purpose this sermon has been preached. Both great ones and small ones should exert themselves, and should in the end gain [true] knowledge. And this manner of acting should be what? Of long duration! For the spiritual good will grow the growth, and will grow exceedingly; at the least it will grow one size and a half.

"This sermon has been preached by the departed.

"Two hundred and fifty years have elapsed since the departure of the teacher."[3]

Mysticism

Did early Buddhism "relegate mysticism to the regions of fairy-tale," as some have asserted?

"There is no such charity as the charity which springeth from virtue [Dharma], which is the inti-

[1] Rock Edict, No. X., Burnouf. [2] Second Separate Edict, Burnouf.
[3] Rupnâth Rock, Bühler.

mate knowledge of virtue [Dharma], the inheritance of virtue [Dharma], the close union with virtue [Dharma]."[1]

"The beloved of the gods, King Piyadasi, honours all forms of religious faith, whether professed by ascetics [pavajitâni] or householders [gahathâni]."[2]

"Whatever villages with their inhabitants may be given or maintained for the sake of the worship, the devotees shall receive the same; and for an example unto my people, they shall exercise solitary austerities."[3]

"And he who acts in conformity with this edict shall be united with Sugato."[4]

Dharma has been translated "the Law," "Virtue," "Thought," "Righteousness," by various scholars. Let the Buddhists give their own translation in their ritual. "I salute that *Dharma* who is *Prajñâ Pâramitâ* (the Wisdom of the Other Bank)."[5]

Now, it seems easy enough for bishops and Boden Professors of Sanskrit to explain away Buddha. He was an atheist. He "professed to know nothing of spirit as distinct from bodily organism."[6] He had "no religion" (p. xxviii); "no prayer" (p. xxviii); no "idea of original sin" (p. 114). He had no real morality, merely "monk morality" (p. 125). He "could not inculcate piety" (p. 124). All these statements may be and are accepted by many readers, but how are we to explain away Aśoka? A king who professed to be specially Buddha's pupil, and by the aid

[1] Edict XII., Prinsep. [2] Rock Edict, No. XII., Wilson.
[3] Delhi Pillar, Edict IV., Prinsep.
[4] Delhi Pillar, Prinsep. [5] Baptismal Ritual of Nepâl.
[6] Sir Monier Monier-Williams, *Buddhism*, p. 105.

of a chisel and hard stone has placed beyond a doubt what he thought upon the subject of Buddha's religion. Could Cartouche build up a Fenelon? Could a Wilberforce develop himself prompted chiefly by a robust admiration of the president of the Hell-Fire Club?

It may be confidently affirmed that there is nothing in the world's history like the *Dharma Râj* of King Aśoka. Imagine Napoleon and Fenelon rolled into one. He antedates Wilberforce in the matter of slavery. He antedates Howard in his humanity towards prisoners. He antedates Tolstoi in his desire to turn the sword into a pruning-hook. He antedates Rousseau, St. Martin, Fichte, in their wish to make interior religion the all in all.

Here are two passages from his edicts that go beyond anything to be seen in any modern State.

"Piyadasi, the friend of the Devas, attaches less importance to alms and outside rites than to his desire to witness the spread of interior religion." [1]

"Progress in *Dharma* may be obtained in two manners—by formal rules, and by the feelings that they help to arouse in the heart. In this double influence the first has a very inferior value, the inner quickening is what is really important." [2]

This is what he would have said at the Czar's Peace Congress:

"Piyadasi, the friend of the Devas, values alone the harvest of the next world. For this alone has this inscription been chiselled, that our sons and our grandsons should make no new conquests. Let them not think that conquests by the sword merit the name of conquests. Let them see their ruin, confusion, and

[1] Edict XIII., Senart. [2] Delhi Pillar, Edict VIII., Senart.

violence. True conquests alone are the conquests of *Dharma*."[1]

Other Reforms

"Formerly, in the great refectory and temple of King Piyadasi, the friend of the Devas, many hundred thousand animals were daily sacrificed for the sake of food meat, . . . but now the joyful chorus resounds again and again that henceforward not a single animal shall be put to death."[2]

"If a man is subject to slavery and ill-treatment, from this moment he shall be delivered by the king from this and other captivity. Many men in this country suffer in captivity, therefore the stûpa containing the commands of the king has been a great want."[3]

But King Aśoka's Edicts throw a strong light upon one very important point indeed—the date of the rise of monks in the sense of housed sedentary idlers. This point I myself have overlooked in my early examination of these inscriptions.

Aśoka's word for the Buddhist monks is *Pavajitâni.* This means houseless ascetics. The Sanskrit word for a monastery is *Saugharâma,* the Garden of the Monks. In point of fact, in the earliest days the monastery was a forest.

"Everywhere the heaven-beloved Râja Piyadasi's double system of medical aid is established, both medical aid for man and medical aid for animals. . . . And wherever there is not such provision, in all such places it is to be prepared and planted, both root

[1] Edict No. XIV., Senart. [2] Rock Edict, No. I., Prinsep.
[3] Dhauli Edict, No. I., Prinsep.

drugs and herbs. Wheresover there is not a provision of them, in all such places shall they be deposited and planted. And in the public highways wells are to be dug and trees to be planted for the accommodation of men and animals."

If we call to mind that in Buddhist countries like Tibet the monasteries are still the only hostelries, and the monks the only doctors, it is plain that the trees here mentioned to be planted along the high-road are for sacred groves or *Saugharâmas.*

Here is another inscription:

"Whenever devotees shall abide around or circumambulate the holy fig-tree for the performance of pious acts, the benefit and pleasure of the country and its inhabitants shall be in making offerings, and according to their generosity or otherwise they shall enjoy prosperity or adversity; and they shall give thanks for the coming of the faith. Whatever villages with their inhabitants may be given or maintained for the sake of the worship, the devotees shall receive the same, and for the example of my people they shall exercise solitary austerities. And likewise whatever blessings they shall pronounce, by these shall my devotees accumulate for the worship. Furthermore, the people in the night shall attend the great myrobalan-tree and the holy fig-tree. My people shall accumulate the great myrobalan-tree (*Terminalia chebula*). My devotees doing thus for the pleasure and profit of the village, whereby they, coming around the beauteous and holy fig-tree, may cheerfully abide in the performance of pious acts."[1]

[1] Delhi Pillar, Edict IV., Prinsep.

If we put two and two together, these passages throw light on the monastery question at the date of Aśoka. The *Saugharâma* was a holy grove with an adjoining village. The grove was peopled with ascetics, performing their dreamy *yoga* under trees "for the benefit of the village." These seem very different, at first sight, from Buddha's *Parivrâjikas*, who were not allowed to stay more than one night in one place, but Buddha's commands were probably addressed to fully enlightened *Bhikshus*, not postulants.

We must bear in mind the problem that Aśoka had to solve:

1. Having conquered India, he required a vast army of enlightened *Bhikshus* to wean it to Buddhism.

2. This vast army had to be fed. Hence the villages and the daily food offerings to the *Muni*, then and now the crucial virtue of the laity. Hence the very extensive plantations of mangoes, banyan-trees, etc. Some verses in the *Sutta Nipâta* illustrate Aśoka:

"Let the Muni, after going about for alms, repair to the outskirt of the wood. Let him sit down near the root of a tree."[1]

The Eighth Edict of Aśoka talks of the mango groves and the banyan-trees that the king had planted along the roads of his dominions. The Queen's Edict on the Allahabad *lat* announces that her gifts of mango gardens, etc., are religious gifts to be credited to her. The inscriptions show, moreover, that the worship in these simple times was imposing and grand. It was night worship in a leafy cathedral, with the stars of heaven as lamps. Three grand

[1] *Nalaka Sutta*, v. 708. "Trees, caves, and graveyards" are said to be his home in that early work.

festivals were appointed by the king, dependent on the lunar mansion Tishya. Again, we have night-worship "torches," "elephants," "processions," and other "celestial spectacles."[1] And another point must be accentuated. His houseless monks (*Pavajitâni*) were certainly not the monks of modern Buddhist convents, contemplative monks not allowed to speak at all. "The increase of converts is the lustre of religion," says the king in the Twelfth Edict.

"For a very long time there have been no ministers of religion who, intermingling among all unbelievers, may overwhelm them with the inundation of religion, and with the abundance of the sacred doctrines. Through Kamboja, Gândhâra, Surashtra, and Petenica, and elsewhere, finding their way unto the uttermost limits of the barbarian countries, for the benefit and pleasure of all . . . are they appointed. Intermingling equally among the dreaded and among the respected both in Pataliputra and in foreign places, teaching better things shall they everywhere penetrate."[2]

Edict XII. enjoins that these teachers are to be very gentle and conciliatory with the "unconverted heretic."

"By such and such conciliatory demeanours shall even the unconverted heretics be propitiated, and such conduct increaseth the number of converted heretics."

"Moreover, hear ye the religion of the faithful, and attend thereto, even such as desire the act, the hope of the beloved of the gods, that all unbelievers may be speedily purified and brought into contentment speedily."[3]

[1] Edict IV., Senart. [2] Edict V., Prinsep. [3] Edict XII., Prinsep.

That the Buddhists were at first wandering beggars without any convents is the opinion of the Russian Orientalist Wassiljew, who supports it from Daranatha's history in Chinese. It asserts that King Ajatasatra passed Varshâ, or Lent, in a graveyard; and that until the date of Upagupta, a contemporary of Aśoka, there were no temples. The first was built at Maṭhurâ.[1]

In *Blackwood's Magazine*, for December 1898, Professor Max Müller writes thus:—

"According to the Divyâ-Vadâna, the guide who undertook to show the king the spots where Buddha had sojourned was Upagupta. He begun by conducting the king to the Garden of Lumbinî, and extending his right hand he said: 'Here, O King, was the Venerable Bhagavat born, and here should be the first monument in honour of the Buddha.'"

Daranatha, who afterwards came to the throne, was Aśoka's grandson, so he ought to be an authority. It is said that Aśoka first raised four stûpas—one where Buddha was born, one where he attained the great enlightenment, one at Benares where he first preached, and one at Kusinagara where he died, a fact confirmed by the archæologists, and also by a passage in the *Mahâ Parinirvâṇa Sûtra.* That Aśoka took over this Brahmin superstition about the stûpa or sepulchral mound proves much and disproves much.

That superstition I have already explained.[2] It was held that a dead man was far more powerful than a living man, and that he might be persuaded to exert this power by flattery and food brought as offerings to

[1] Chap. iv., cited by Wassiljew, *Buddhism*, p. 41.
[2] See Chap. II.

his tomb. In point of fact, all magical rites, and indeed all religious rites—the ideas are not by any means unconnected, are based on this belief. That Aśoka's introduction of the stûpa into Buddhism implies a belief on his part that Buddha was non-existent is of course an absurdity. The stûpa, the relics, the ritual, the entire outside worship are bound intimately together.

The marbles of a Buddhist stûpa, the celebrated Amarâvatî Tope, are on the grand staircase of the British Museum, and two of these I have drawn for my work, *Buddhism in Christendom*. The first represents Buddha and the heavenly host coming down to the worshippers, who have placed a large rice cake upon the altar. The second represents him coming down in the same pomp to the incense smoke. Here is a passage, given by Beal from the Chinese liturgy, which explains what these sculptures mean:

"I regard the sacred altar as a Royal Gem on which the Shadow (spirit) of Śâkya Tathâgata appears."[1]

But before we go any further we must settle the exact position of those whose theories we are considering. Let us take the three most conspicuous believers in Pyrrho-Buddha as the true Buddha. These are Sir Monier Monier-Williams, Dr. Oldenburg, and Professor Rhys Davids, but these authorities are unanimous in little beyond that one point. Dr. Oldenburg rejects the second convocation, for the sufficient reason that there is no record of it in the Northern literature. He accepts, however, the first convocation and a vast early Buddhist literature, but holds that the early Buddhists dwelt not in monasteries but under trees.

[1] Beal, *Catena of Buddhist Scriptures*, p. 243.

Sir Monier Monier-Williams, on the other hand, accepts the second convocation, but will have nothing to say to the first and its vast library, on the grounds that the letters of the alphabet were not at that time known in India, and that the holy books in Ceylon were not committed to writing until the date of King Wattaginini (B.C. 104–76). He also holds that it is flying in the face of all evidence to maintain that the Mahâyâna never reached Ceylon.[1] Of the three Orientalists, these two last show themselves the most critical, but Professor Rhys Davids is certainly the most logical.

To prove Buddha an atheist, he holds that a chain of circumstantial evidence is required, every link of which is vital.

A Ceylon uncontaminated by the Mahâyâna is the first requisite, a Ceylon that received from Mahinda the vast literature four times as voluminous as our Bible, which was made canonical at the Council of Râjâgṛiha, and reaffirmed at the Council of Patna.

To prove all this, implicit reliance must be placed in Buddhaghosa and his collection of Southern scriptures (Aṭṭha Kathâ), especially in his Life of Buddha, the best authority we have,—in fact, the only one that is of any authority at all. Here, again, he is opposed by Sir Monier Monier-Williams, who says that in the Southern literature there is not a single biography of Buddha worthy of the name.[2]

But these theories of Professor Rhys Davids will not bear a moment's historical investigation. From Hwen Thsang we see that Ceylon was the hotbed of the Mahâyâna movement.

[1] *Buddhism*, p. 30. [2] *Ibid.* p. 18.

"In Ceylon," he says, "are about ten thousand monks who follow the doctrines of the Great Vehicle."[1] He says also that Deva Bodhisatwa, a Cingalese monk, was one of its most active expositors.[2] At Kanchapura the Chinese pilgrim came upon three hundred monks that had just fled across the sea from Ceylon to escape the anarchy and famine consequent on the death of a Ceylon king. As Hwen Thsang afterwards presided at a great convocation summoned by King Siluditya to attack the Little Vehicle, he, if anybody, would know the difference between the two sects.

As to Buddhaghosa, he was alive about the time that Fa Hian, the Chinese traveller, visited India. He was a converted Brahmin sent by the great monastery at Magadha to Ceylon to retranslate into Pali and re-edit all the Cingalese literature, a feat that he accomplished in a sweeping way. He was a rank Pyrrho-Buddhist, and Fa Hian records an important fact. At this date the great convent of Magadha was the head-quarters of the "Great Vehicle" movement. He calls it "the very lofty and very beautiful Great Vehicle Monastery."[3]

But in point of fact, can any one who has read this short chapter believe in Pyrrho-Buddha prompting King Aśoka? Can they believe in the first convocation at Râjâgṛiha, or the second at Patna? To these convocations Aśoka deals a straighter blow.

The old history of Ceylon, the Mahawanso, announces that King Aśoka was puzzled with the question: "Of what religion was Sugato?" which word Mr. Turnour renders "the Deity of Happy Advent." In conse-

[1] Hwen Thsang, *Histoire*, p. 192.

[2] *Mémoires*, vol. i. pp. 218, 277.

[3] *Pilgrimage*, p. 254.

quence he determined to summon a council of all the monks of Jambudwipa, to be presided over by Moggaliputra. The Ninth Edict talks of "consultations upon matters of religion" (Senart's translation). The Third Edict talks of an *Anusamyâna* (general assembly). The convocation is dated by scholars, B.C. 244. Certainly the following inscription seems to give us its results:

"It is well know, sirs, to what lengths have gone my respect for and faith in Buddha, Dharma, Sañgha. All that our Lord Buddha has spoken is well spoken. Wherefore, sirs, it must indeed be regarded as having indisputable authority. So the true faith shall last long. Thus, my lords, I honour with the highest honour those religious works, *Vinayasamaka* ("Lessons in Discipline"), *Aryavasas* ("the Supernatural Powers of the Aryas"), *Anâgatabhayas* ("the Terrors of the Future"), *Munigâthas* ("the Metrical Life of Buddha"), *Upatisapasina* ("the Questions of Upatishya"), *Moneyasûta* ("the Sûtra on the Inner Life"), and the *Admonition to Râhula concerning Falsehood uttered by our Lord Buddha.* These religious works, sir, I would that the *Bhikshus* and *Bhikshunis*, for the advancement of their good name, shall uninterruptedly study and remember."[1]

This is the inscription, and it is difficult to see how any Orientalist or any non-Orientalist can undervalue its importance. Would Aśoka have had "doubts" and "consultations" as to what Buddha had taught, if a literature four times as copious as the Christian's Bible was already received as canonical? And supposing that the canon was fixed before his time, why should he reject the greater part of it, and only require about

[1] Second Bairât Rock.

1 per cent. of the whole to be learnt and chanted out by his monks and nuns? The "Question of Upatishya" has come down to us, and also the "Admonition to Râhula regarding Falsehood."[1] The two together would be about as long as the Epistle to Philemon in the Bible, and the Life of Buddha was also probably very short. I used this argument in an early work, and it was thus answered by Professor Rhys Davids in the *Saturday Review*:

"His argument, from the titles in the Aśoka monuments, cannot be seriously urged when we know that they are rather descriptions of contents than fixed titles, and may be easily varied."

Now, with every desire to do justice to an opponent's argument, I own that here I am fairly puzzled. Is not every "fixed title," in design at least, a description of the "contents of the work"? Is it conceivable that an intelligent king, having summoned a religious convocation from the most distant ends of his vast dominions to draw up a catalogue of the books to be considered sacred, should deliberately order that no fixed title should be used. Imagine the Council of Laodicea, when settling the New Testament Canon, forbidden to use such titles as the "Acts of the Apostles" or the "Gospel according to Matthew," and forced to adopt some novel and unknown heading which was not to be a "title."

Moreover, is it a fact that Aśoka's seven tractates had no fixed titles? Let us consider the "Question of Upatishya."

Upatishya had one supreme fear, the fear of death. One day, in company with Maudgalyâyana (they were

[1] See p. 87.

both seekers of truth), they witnessed a festival from a hilltop. "See," said Upatishya, "in two hundred years all these living beings will be the prey of death. If there is a principle of destruction, can there not also be a principle of life?"

This was the "Question of Upatishya," and he propounded it to many teachers, but none solved it satisfactorily until he came across Athadzi, a disciple who expounded to him Buddha's Dharma.

Here the title is plainly the real title; the same must be said of the Metrical Life of Buddha, the treatise on Discipline; and, in fact, of all the seven works mentioned in the Second Bairât Rock. Dr. Oldenburg, in treating this subject, is more intelligible than Professor Rhys Davids, but certainly he is not so cautious. He holds that the seven tractates mentioned on the Second Bairât Rock are only a portion of the vast literature that Mahinda carried to Ceylon; but as the memory of the monks was the sole vehicle by which Buddhist literature in those days could be handed down, who committed to memory the remaining literature?—about 99 per cent. of the whole. Aśoka's monks and nuns were ordered all of them to learn up and chant the seven Aśoka tractates and no others. Mahinda crossed to Ceylon with four monks and one layman, as the *Mahâwanso* tells us. Did this layman carry in his brain the rest of the literature, four times as copious as the Christian Scriptures. Mahinda left one year after the convocation. The layman in this case must have been a quick learner with a very good memory.

It is high time that Aśoka were properly studied. Orientalists have been meritoriously industrious over the accents of some of the inscriptions and the want of accents upon others. They have differentiated the letters, "Northern Aśoka" and "Southern Aśoka." They have cavilled over the words, poor chisel scratches worn down by the centuries. Let us hope they will now get to the sentences. I myself plead guilty to having undervalued Aśoka. When I first read him I found in his "Stûpa of Commandment," his "proclamations by beat of drum," a little too much of—what shall I say—the conquering general-officer. He insisted on marching his subjects to Swarga in orderly time.

"Never was there in any former period a system of instruction applicable to every season and to every action, such as is that which is now established by me."[1]

In another edict he states that similar arrangements for spreading religion "have not been known for many hundred years."

Then, in the First Dhauli Edict, he tells his *rajukas* that his chief desire is to spread the religion of Buddha:

"Now, the chief means for effecting this are the instructions that I give to you. You are placed over hundreds of thousands of human beings to win the affection of the well-behaved. Every man is my child, and my wish is that my children may enjoy all sorts of prosperity in this world, and happiness in the next. I have the same desire for all men."

"It is in this design," says the Eighth Edict, "that I have set up this inscription, that it may be read by my sons and grandsons, and endure as long as the moon and the sun, that they may follow my teaching and obtain happiness in this world and the next."[2]

[1] Edict VI., Prinsep.

[2] Senart's translation.

"Thus shall the heaven-born king cause Dharma to flourish."[1]

I own that this sort of writing again prejudiced me against the king when, for this, my new work, I returned to the study of the inscriptions. "The good king writes as if he were writing a Bible!" Thus ran my thoughts.

Then came a sudden flash of intelligence. What if the king was writing a Bible! At once I seized Sir Alexander Cunningham's *Corpus Inscriptionum Indicarum* for dates. I read:

"Earliest Rock Edicts . . B.C. 251
Synod under Mogaliputra . B.C. 244"

There it was plain, enough. Aśoka's inscriptions were the first Buddhist teachings committed to writing, the first authoritative Buddhist scriptures.

This meant much. It proved, to begin with, that I had done injustice to Aśoka in charging him with an arrogant usurpation of the office of the Buddhist hierarchy. He was merely setting forth to the best of his literary ability the tenets of a religious teacher who had changed his life. He says that no such instruction had been given before, because, in point of fact, it had not. He says that his teaching will give happiness in this world and bliss in the next, meaning simply that it was Buddha's *Dharma*. Far from usurping the office of a Buddhist hierarchy, he was in fact helping to create one. His *rajukas* and overseers were apparently civil officers and laymen, but they were paving the way for bishops and superior monks,—in fact, that hierarchy which Bishop Bigandet has pronounced to be pin for pin similar to that of the Church of Rome.

[1] Edict IV.

He established a council or "conference on religion," that the few poor scraps of Buddhist tradition should be saved from oblivion. Here was the Buddhist Bible in embryo. He changed a cairn or two into elaborate Buddhist *stûpas* and, for good or ill, created the temple. His rest-houses and the mango groves that he planted to save the dreaming *yogi* from the sun became by and by elaborate monasteries. The Nagarjuni inscriptions by Aśoka's grandson, Daranatha, announce that he gave the Gopi's Cave and the "well-cavern" to the dreaming *bhadantas* in perpetuity. This reveals much. Buddha had forbidden his beggars the use of a house. With pardonable Jesuitism, it was now argued that a cavern was not a house.

CHAPTER VIII

PYRRHO-BUDDHA

WE now come to Pyrrho-Buddha. The evidence regarding his introduction is far more complete than the evidence of the introduction of some of the leading novelties into the Roman Catholic Church; for instance, transubstantiation. Pyrrho-Buddha and the "Great Vehicle" teaching, as it was called, was officially recognised at the convocation summoned by King Kaniśka about A.D. 16.

From Fa Hian, the Chinese traveller, who visited India in the fourth century, we will copy down what the "Great Vehicle" reformers said of themselves. The controversy between the "Vehicles" was illustrated by an allegory. Three vehicles once crossed a river. The first, drawn by a sheep, was the "Little Vehicle," or early Buddhism, and the sheep looked timorously towards the "other bank." The second vehicle was drawn by a stag, who showed more courage. He looked back, after the manner of stags when the hunter's arrows are assailing his does. But the third, or "Great Vehicle," was drawn by the lordly elephant. He marched on sure ground.

Here is the controversy in a nutshell. The "other bank" is the Hindoo phrase for heaven, which was supposed to be separated from earth by the river

Vaitaranî. The early Buddhists looked forward to the continuation of the individuality in Swarga. This was pronounced by the new teachers to be the "Pride of Individuality" (*Âtmamada*); and Hwen Thsang records how a foolish monk of the "Little Vehicle" was sternly rebuked by the great Maitreya himself for holding it.[1] The philosophy of the reformers (most philosophies are simple contradictions of certain current views) proclaimed that mighty Nothingness (*Mahâ Śunya*) was the goal of the truly enlightened mystic. Buddha was dethroned. His relics were thrown out of the stûpas. And the white statue of Bodhisatwa Maitreya, the coming Buddha, replaced him on the altar.

The worship of a Bodhisatwa seems at first sight the worship conceived by a madman. The main design of the *Lalita Vistara* is to show how a Bodhisatwa is to develop into a Buddha. The Bodhisatwa is in the heaven Tuśita. He is still in the Kâmaloca, or Domain of Appetite. His "Divine eye" is still closed. Far from being the Governor of the Universe, for it was thus Maitreya got to be viewed, he can do no good thing. And yet the great allegory is full of interpolated passages which call the "Buddhas of the Ten Horizons" the "Bodhisatwas of the Ten Horizons," and so on. The absurdity reaches its culminating point when, in the Nepâlese litany, although it is entitled the "Praise of the Seven Buddhas," an address to an eighth Buddha, Maitreya, is added. And as ritual is a more conservative institution than metaphysic, some other marked inconsistencies were found necessary. The corpse-worship of the old Buddhism had to be retained, because that was the outward rite

[1] *Mémoires*, tome i. p. 222.

of Buddhism. But as the prophet that has not yet come to the world is not yet available as a corpse, sepulchral mounds had to be erected, that contained neither corpses nor relics. The Bodhisatwa, or future Buddha, had many stûpas erected to him. They contained no relics, but the disciples of the "Vehicle that drives to the Great Nowhere" offered flowers and food to the non-existent relics. They marched three times round the stûpa, within the mystic altar rails. On the Ganges, Hwen Thsang was seized by pirates. These, struck by his splendid physique, prepared to sacrifice him to the goddess Durgâ. The pilgrim prayed to Maitreya, and suddenly, aloft in the sky, "in the palace of the Tuśita heaven," the dazzling form of the Bodhisatwa appeared. He was seated on a throne with legions of spirits around him. A mighty tempest suddenly arose, which whirled the dust into huge spiral clouds, and sank all the pirates' boats. They repented, and released the pilgrim.[1] Fa Hian, in a mighty storm at sea, also nearly lost his life. He prayed to Bodhisatwa Avalokiteśvara, and the ship was saved.[2]

At Maṭhurâ, during his visit, as the pilgrim Hwen Thsang shows, this rival stûpa-worship was very marked. The disciples of the Little Vehicle paid homage to the relics of Sâriputra, Maudgalyâyana, Ânanda, and the other great Buddhist saints, who had each one a handsome stûpa in that city. But the disciples of the Great Vehicle worshipped the Bodhisatwas, says the Chinese pilgrim.[3] Fa Hian bears similar testimony.[4]

[1] Hwen Thsang, *Histoire*, p. 118.
[2] Fa Hian, p. 359.
[3] Hwen Thsang, *Histoire*, p. 104.
[4] *Pilgrimage*, p. 101.

If a vast nation of subtle thinkers were suddenly called upon to choose between the teachings of a prophet of the past, and those of a prophet yet unborn, one would think that the teachings of the former would have the preference, as they would certainly be better available to the general public. How the quaint cultus of a man who was only to attain the spiritual enlightenment some thousands of years hence arose, it is very difficult now to say precisely. We see from the writings of Hwen Thsang, that from its political side the movement was aimed against the authority of the Âchârya of Magadha, the Rome of the Buddhists. Kaniśka, a powerful Kashmîri, had conquered vast territories that included Hindû Kush, and Kabul, Yarkand and Khokan, Kashmîr and Ladâk, the plains of the Upper Ganges as far as Agra, the Punjâb, Rajputâna, Guzerat, and Scinde. Such a large Buddhist empire would require a strengthened discipline amongst its great army of monks. Magadha was not included in this empire, and the two leading monks of Kaniśka, Pârśvika and Vasubandhu, may have wished to establish an ecclesiastical authority independent of the "High Priest of all the World," as the Âchârya of Magadha is called in the *Mahâwanso*.[1] Perhaps the authority of the latter was ill defined; and perhaps it had also become weakened, now that Magadha was no longer the headquarters of a large empire. If a strong religious controversy were raging, it would be the manifest policy of the king's head ecclesiastics to take the side that opposed the Âchârya ("Teacher" *par excellence*) of Magadha. The leader of the re-

[1] *Mahâwanso*, p. 21.

ligious movement was a monk of the convent of Ayodhyâ—a visionary, one Asaṅgha, who was transported one night to the heaven Tuśita, and received the Yoga Śâstra, the principal scripture of the new faith, from Maitreya himself. Vasubandhu, his pupil, was also an author. He indited many of the chief Śâstras of the innovating Buddhism.[1] He presided at the convocation summoned by King Kaniśka to introduce it. The king wanted to hold the convocation at Magadha:

"He wished to repair to Râjâgṛiha, to the stone palace where Kaśyapa had formed the collection of sacred books. But the honourable Pârśvika (his senior monk) said to him: 'Take care, in that city are many heretics! Many conflicting opinions will be expressed, and we shall not have time to answer and refute them. Why compose Śâstras? The whole convocation is attached to this kingdom. Your realms are defended on all sides by high mountains, under the guardianship of Yakshas.'"[2]

It is plain from this that the new creed was established in the teeth of the High Priest of Magadha and the official Buddhism; but Magadha afterwards took it up, as its tendency was plainly in the direction of strengthening the priesthood. At the date of King Śîlâditya the Âchârya of Magadha, in his headquarters at Nalanda, was the chief exponent of the new creed.

I will copy down two passages from Hwen Thsang. This is what the disciples of the Little Vehicle said of their opponents:

"They answered that the heretics of the Carriage

[1] Hwen Thsang, *Histoire*, p. 114 et seq.

[2] Hwen Thsang, *Memoires*, vol. i. p. 174.

that drives to the Great Nowhere [Śunyapushpa], residing at the monastery of Nalanda, differed in nothing from the Kâpâlikas."[1]

They said, too, that the doctrine of the Great Vehicle did not come from Buddha at all.[2]

A Kâpâlika was a Brahmin, cunning in Tântric rites. A drama—the Prabodha Chandra Udaya—gives us a sketch of him when Buddhism was the official religion of India. Talking to a Buddhist, he speaks thus:—

> "With goodly necklace decked of bones of men,
> Haunting the tombs, from cups of human skulls
> Eating and quaffing, ever I behold,
> With eyes that meditation's salve hath cleared,
> The world of diverse jarring elements
> Composed, but still all one with the Supreme.

The Buddhist.—This man professes the rule of a Kâpâlika. I will ask him what it is (*going to him*). O ho, you with the bone and skull necklace!—what are your hopes of happiness and salvation?

The Adept.—Wretch of a Buddhist! Well, hear what is our religion:—

> With flesh of men, with brain and fat well smeared,
> We make our grim burnt offering—break our fast
> From cups of holy Brahmin's skull, and ever
> With gurgling drops of blood that plenteous stream
> From hard throats quickly cut; by us is worshipped
> With human offerings meet the dread Bhairava.
>
> . . . .
>
> I call at will the best of gods, great Hari,
> And Hara's self and Brahma. I restrain
> With my sole voice the course of stars that wander
> In heaven's bright vault; the earth, with all its load
> Of mountains, fields, and cities, I at will
> Reduce once more to water; and, behold,
> I drink it up!"[3]

---

[1] Hwen Thsang, *Memoires*, p. 220. [2] *Ibid.*

[3] *Journ. Beng. As. Soc.* vol. vi. p. 15.

The Kâpâlika, or Adept, plainly thought that he was God on earth; that at will he could restrain the movement of the stars and destroy the universe. Plainly, in the view of the early Buddhist school, the movement entitled the Great Vehicle was in the direction of turning the humble "Son of Śâkya" into a pretentious Kâpâlika. In early Buddhism any one, without the intervention of any other mortal, could make a direct appeal to the supreme Buddha merely by walking three times round a relic stûpa. But Hwen Thsang plainly tells us that the apostles of the Great Vehicle discouraged this worship of Śâkya Muni and the dead saints.

What was the inner cultus of the Śunyavâdi stated with philosophical precision. If we could recall and cross-examine a candid professor of the creed, he would no doubt tell us that the worship of the babe unborn, the Glad Tidings of Flat Contradiction, and the tomb-worship without human remains, were mere outside accidents. Rajendra Lala Mitra, the prince of modern Orientalists, in his *Nepâlese Buddhist Literature*, affirms that the philosophy of the *Mahâyâna* was a servile theft from contemporary Brahmin tractates. The Bible of the Śunyavâdis was the *Rakshâ Bhagavatî*. Brian Hodgson confirms this.[1] The Hindoo writer tells us that the *Rakshâ Bhagavatî* is an avowed attack on Hinayâna, or "Little Vehicle," which is "refuted repeatedly" — or early Buddhism, in point of fact.[2] Let us see if this work for the first time in Buddhism preaches a God and immortal life. That is the contention of Professor Rhys

[1] *Literature of Nepal*, p. 16.
[2] Rajendra Lala Mitra, *Nepâlese Buddhist Literature*, p. 178.

Davids. I will give the titles of some of its chapters.

Chap. I. The subject of Nothingness (Sunyata) expounded.

Chap. II. Relation of the soul to form, colour, and vacuity.

Chap. IV. Relation of form to vacuity.

Chap. VII. How a Bodhisatwa merges all natural attributes into vacuity.

Chap. XII. The doctrine of Mahâyâna and its advantages, derived principally, if not entirely, from its recognition of the greatness of Śunyavâda (Nihilistic doctrine of the Brahmin sect of Śunyavâdis).

Chap. XIII. To the Bodhisatwa there is nothing eternal, nothing transient, nothing painful, nothing pleasant. All qualities are unreal as a dream.

Chaps. XIV.–XVI. The principle of the *Prajñâ Pâramitâ* imparted by Buddha to Indra. The end sought is the attainment of vacuity.

Chap. XXXV. All objects attainable by the study of Nihilism.[1]

Hodgson gives a bit of what he calls this "pure Pyrrhonism" from the same book. Buddha is made to talk thus:

"The being of all things is derived from belief, reliance, in this order: from false knowledge, delusive impression; from delusive impression, general notions; from them, particulars; from them, the six seats of the senses; from them, contact; from it, definite sensation and perception; from it, thirst or desire; from it, embryolic (physical) existence; from it, birth or actual existence; from it, all the distinctions of genus and

[1] *Nepâlese Buddhist Literature*, p. 180.

species among animate things; from them, decay and death, after the manner and period peculiar to each. Such is the procession of all things into existence from delusion (avidyâ), and in the inverse order to that of their procession they retrograde into non-existence" (p. 79).

Sir Monier Monier-Williams gives a sketch of early Buddhism almost in the same words:

"The universe around us, with all its visible phenomena, must be recognised as an existing entity, for we see before our eyes evidence of its actual existence. But it is an entity produced out of nonentity, and destined to lapse again into nonentity when its time is fulfilled. For out of Nothingness it came, and into Nothingness it must return."[1]

Has the Boden Professor of Sanskrit here remembered the passage from Brian Hodgson, and forgotten in his mind that it is not by a writer on early Buddhism, but by one who proposed to "refute repeatedly" all early Buddhist ideas?

Sir Monier Monier-Williams derives Buddha's atheism from the Brahmajâla Sûtra, the brief of so many modern writers on Buddhism. This little work is more rank in its Pyrrho-Buddhism than even the "Diamond Cutter." The title means the "Net of the Brahmins," and it professes to refute "sixty-two heterodox sects," which it does by contradicting everybody and everything, something in this style: The universe is finite and infinite, the soul is eternal and non-eternal, man remembers his past lives and yet never remembers them, existence is the result of a previously existent cause and is not the result of anything of the sort. Sir Monier Monier-Williams, on the strength of a state-

[1] *Buddhism*, p. 118.

ment that no Gods are eternal,[1] pronounces Buddha an atheist, and yet in one part of the Sûtra there is a great deal about Brahma's heaven and Brahma himself which in Buddha's day were both deemed eternal. Professor Rhys Davids, on the other hand, fastens on three speeches which I here transcribe:

"Priests among these Samanas and Brahmins are some who hold the doctrine of future conscious existence, and in sixteen modes teach that the soul consciously exists after death. But the teaching of these Samanas and Brahmins is founded on their ignorance, their want of perception of truth, their own personal experience, and on the fluctuating emotions of those who are under the influence of their passions.

"Priests among these Samanas and Brahmins are some who hold the doctrine of future unconscious existence, and in eight modes teach that the soul exists after death in a state of unconsciousness. But the teaching of these Samanas and Brahmins is founded on their ignorance, their want of perception of truth, their own personal experience, and on the fluctuating emotions of those who are under the influence of their passions.

"Priests among these Samanas and Brahmins are some who hold the doctrine of a future state of being neither conscious nor yet unconscious, and in eight modes teach that the soul will hereafter exist in a state between consciousness and unconsciousness. But the teaching of these Samanas and Brahmins is founded on their ignorance, their want of perception of truth, their own personal experience, and on the

[1] *Buddhism*, p. 106.

fluctuating emotions of those who are under the influence of their passions."

Plainly, says the professor, conscious existence after death, unconscious existence after death, and existence in a state that is "neither conscious nor unconscious" are here flatly denied. "Would it be possible," he adds triumphantly, "in a more complete and categorical manner to deny that there is any soul, or anything of any kind which continues to exist in any manner after death?"

But there is a fourth passage, apparently overlooked by the professor, which flatly contradicts the other three:

"Priests among these Samanas and Brahmins are some who affirm that existence is destroyed, and who in seven modes teach that existing beings are cut off, destroyed, annihilated. But the teaching of these Samanas and Brahmins is founded on their ignorance, their want of perception of truth, their own personal experience, and on the fluctuating emotions of those who are under the influence of their passions."[1]

It must be mentioned, too, that the *Sûtra* talks of monasteries with monks indulging in "large elevated beds," "embroidered counterpanes," "cushions ornamented with gold and embroidery"; which carries it a long way from Aśoka, and still further from Buddha, who, by the way, as a Brahmin could scarcely have had a revelation of the *Śunyavâdi's* philosophy made to him. In his day there was no toleration, and the Brahmins objected to unorthodox fancies about the supreme Brahma.

[1] Grimblot, *Sept Suttas Pâlis*, p. 107.

Dethronement of Pyrrho-Buddha

We now plunge into a tangle of uncertainties tempered by one very prominent fact—Pyrrho-Buddha was promptly dethroned. The "Ever-living Buddha" (*Buddha Amitâyas*) was set up in his place with an eternal "Paradise of Pure Bliss" (*Sukhâvatî*).

The chief difficulty about *Amitâyas* is the fact that the *Sûtras* that relate to him are bound up with the *Sûtras* that set up and set forth Pyrrho-Buddha. The learned amongst the Chinese and the learned amongst the Nepâlese call both *Mahâyâna* literature. And Professor Max Müller, in his *Sacred Books of the East*, has bound up under the same title the "Diamond Cutter," which builds up Pyrrho-Buddha and the *Sûtra* about *Sukhâvatî* which demolishes him.

For philosophies are destructive more often than constructive. The calm philosopher aims his new shaft at some current idea that disturbs his calmness. The Pyrrho-Buddhist proclaimed that there was no God except Nothingness, no heaven except Nothingness, no blissful future for man except Nothingness. Life was a sickly dream of bright suns and green fields and human joys and human sorrows, but bright suns and green fields and human joys were non-existent. Nothing was real except the sorrow. As an emphatic protest against all this, the demolisher proclaimed an eternal God, eternal heavens, and an eternal life for man, blissful when he had attained the great awakening. To name his God he picked out the strongest words in the Sanskrit dictionary—*A*, privative; *mṛita*, death; *Âyus*, life: Amitâyas, the "Buddha of Deathless Life." The word Buddha was given to this god as an emphatic protest against the theory of the Pyrrho-Buddhist, that all the Buddhas had gone to the blissful *Nirvâṇa* of Nothingness. And as a protest against the dreary pessimism that held all life—the higher life as well as the lower—to be pure misery, it called its Paradise the "Joyful Place."

Who were those demolishers, and when did they live? There we are at fault. We have seen that the Pyrrho-Buddhist described himself and his opponents in a little allegory about three "Chariots." Was the Middle Chariot, *Mâdhyamika*, the "Vehicle" of the worshippers of Amitâyas? If the Pyrrho-Buddhist could be credited with strict logic, this conclusion is difficult. The "Great Chariot," with its lordly elephant, had a supreme contempt for the miserable creatures in the "Little Chariot," who sighed for prolonged individuality in an eternal heaven. The Middle Chariotiers, on the other hand, are described as being more noble than this,—they have some thoughts for their neighbours. But the worshippers of Amitâyas had certainly also the desire of a blissful hereafter, and a prolongation of the individuality in an eternal *Sukhâvatî*, and they certainly proclaimed this more loudly than the early Buddhists in their "Little Chariot."

That this sweeping antagonism between the Pyrrho-Buddhists and the Anti-Pyrrho-Buddhists should have remained unnoticed by several generations of Orientalists is one of the curiosities of literature, considering that, by a quaint freak of historical evolution, there are alive now millions of human beings who bear overwhelming witness to it. The absurdities of Pyrrho-Buddhism broke up the Buddhist ascendency in India. Brahminism revived, and drove one half of the Buddhists to Ceylon and the south, and the other half to Kashmîr, Nepâl, Tibet.

From this circumstance a very remarkable fact emerges:

All the Buddhists of Ceylon, all the Buddhists of Burmah, all the Buddhists of Siam, are ready to come forward and announce that Pyrrho-Buddhism is the real Buddhism.

On the other hand, even the materialistic school of Northern Buddhism shows the influence of the worshippers of Amitâyas Buddha.

In the matter of Southern Buddhism, I will give here a sketch by a clever Siamese statesman. A few years ago Chao Phya Praklang published a book, which has been partly translated by Mr. Alabaster under the title of *The Modern Buddhist.* Chao Phya Praklang is a clear and bold writer. He announces that Buddhism denies a God and an eternal hereafter. I will condense his views.

There is no God; nothing but an unintelligent causation called *Kam.* If I lead a virtuous life through *Kam,* in my next existence I obtain the reward of riches. If I lead an evil life, in my next rebirth, through pure cause and effect, I may be a pig. If, like Augkuliman, I murder "nine hundred and ninety-nine people," I can "cut off' the *Kam*" of these murders by a saintly life. If as a child I mimic my parents, and bow to a *Prachedi* (spire of a Buddhist *chaitya*), even then I inadvertently store up meritorious *Kam* (*Karma* of the Indian Buddhists).

Now, it is impossible to state more clearly than this the creed of the Pyrrho-Buddhist, that human life comes from unintelligent *Śunya*, or Nothingness, and goes back to Nothingness again. Siam and Burmah got their Buddhism from Ceylon, and Ceylon got its philosophy from the frantic Pyrrho-Buddhist Buddhaghosa.

As a contrast to all this, let us turn to the Northern Buddhism, as revealed to Brian Hodgson by that invaluable Buddhist, Amirta Nanda Bandhya. Amongst the Northern Buddhists there are four great schools of philosophy. The first, the *Aiswarikas*, believe in a "supreme, infinite, and self-existent Deity." The second, the *Swâbhâvikas*, are materialists. Matter, they hold, is eternal, "and so are the powers of matter, which powers possess not only activity, but intelligence."[1] The two other schools—the *Karmikas* and the *Yâtnikas*—are said to be comparatively modern, and are chiefly modifications of the *Aiswarika* school.

Amitâyas, or Amitâbha, is the popular Buddha of Tibet and China. In Japan even the Shinto believers have adopted him.

"I adore Tathâgata Amitâbha, who dwells in the Buddha region Devachan." This is from the ritual of Tibet.[2]

"One in spirit respectfully we invoke thee. Hail! Amitâbha Lokajit, of the world Sukhâvatî!" This is from the ritual of China.[3]

From the same ritual is the following prayer:—

"Oh, would that our teacher Śâkya Muni, and our merciful Father Amitâbha, would descend to this sacred

[1] Hodgson, *Nepâlese Literature*, p. 23.
[2] Schlangintweit, *Buddhism in Tibet*, p. 129.
[3] *Catena of Buddhist Scriptures*, p. 403.

precinct and be present with us, who now discharge these religious duties. Would that the great, perfect, illimitable, compassionate heart, influenced by these invocations, would now attend and receive our offerings."

I have reserved to the last one more service that King Aśoka has unwittingly rendered to the modern study of Buddhism. It is, as I judge, the crucial one of all. It must be borne in mind that this worthy monarch was impetuous, courageous, self-asserting. In point of fact, in character he was not unlike Buddhaghosa. Both were converted Brahmins. Both possessed the fiery zeal of converts. If the Buddhism of King Aśoka's date had been Pyrrho-Buddhism, would there not be some trace of it in the inscriptions? Or perhaps the question might be better put in this way—Would not Pyrrho-Buddhism have quite deluged the rocks and the *Stambhas*? Imagine for a moment Buddhaghosa in the king's place. Would not his "Stûpas of Commandment" have proclaimed with emphasis that there was no God but the Eternal Nothing, that man has no soul but the Eternal Nothing, and no body to put it in if he had. Would he not have impressed on his subjects the great sin of *atmamada*, or a desire of prolonged life in the next world. It must be remembered, too, that Pyrrho-Buddhism had its outward and visible signs as well as its inward and spiritual grace. These were the worship of Maitreya, and stûpas without relics. Is there any trace of these in King Aśoka's day?

To sum up our deductions from the priceless inscriptions of Aśoka:

1. At his date there were no idle monks living in

buildings. His Bhikshus were missionaries who slept under trees and preached in all lands.

2. His edicts constituted the first Buddhist Bible, and the first documents of the religion that were written down.

3. His convocation was the first attempt on the part of the Buddhists to make up a religious literature. It was limited to the seven tractates mentioned on the Second Bairât Rock.

4. It is absolutely certain that King Aśoka did not believe that Buddha at death ceased to exist, for he took over the leading superstition of the Brahmins of his day, that a dead saint was more powerful than a living saint, and that through his corpse or relics he could perform miracles. In consequence he erected stûpas all over his kingdom, in imitation of the Brahmin stûpas. The Buddhist books are full of the miracles performed by the relics of Buddha.

5. It is also certain that the king's creed was not atheism, and that, far from despising mysticism, he himself went through rigorous ordeals to become "one with Buddha."

6. There is not the least trace of Pyrrho-Buḍḍha at Aśoka's date, nor of the outward indications of the movement, namely, the empty stûpas and sculptures representing Maitreya.

CHAPTER IX

THE APOSTLES OF THE BLOODLESS ALTAR

THERE are two Zoroasters. One of these Zoroasters lived 6000 years B.C. according to Darmesteter, and the other about 500 years B.C. The earlier Zoroaster swathed Persia in a network of silly rites and regulations. A culprit who "threw away a dead dog" was to receive a thousand blows with the horse-goad, and one thousand with the Craosha charana. A culprit who slew a dog with a "prickly back" and a "woolly muzzle" was to receive a similar punishment."[1] This Zoroaster was particular about the number of gnats, ants, lizards that the devout were enjoined to kill.[2] This Zoroaster proclaimed a god who loved to see on his altar a "hundred horses, a thousand cows, ten thousand small cattle," and so on.[3] But the second Zoroaster proclaimed a bloodless altar, and sought to tear the network of the first Zoroaster to shreds. What was the meaning of this? Simply that the Buddhist Wanderers had by this time invaded Persia, and had fastened their doctrines upon the chief local prophet. This was their habit. A study of this second religion, the religion of Mithras, will help us to some of the secrets of Buddhist propagandism.

Mr. Felix Oswald cites Wassiljew as announcing

[1] *Fargard*, xxx. [2] *Ibid.* xiv. [3] *Khordah Avesta*, xii.

that the Buddhist missionaries had reached Western Persia, B.C. 450. This date would, of course, depend on the date of Buddha's life and Buddha's death. The latter is now definitely fixed by Bühler's translation of Aśoka's Rupnâth rock-inscription, B.C. 470. Wassiljew, citing Daranatha, announces that Madeantica, a convert of Ânanda, Buddha's leading disciple, reached Ouchira in Kashmîr. From Kashmîr Buddhism passed promptly to Kandahar and Kabul (p. 40). Thence it penetrated quickly to Bactria, and soon invaded "all the country embraced by the word Turkistan, where it flourished until disturbed by Mahomet."

Tertullian has two passages which describe the religion of Mithras.

He says that the devil, to "pervert the truth," by "the mystic rites of his idols, vies even with the essential portions of the sacraments of God. He, too, baptizes some—that is, his own believers and faithful followers. He promises the putting away of sins by a laver (of his own), and, if my memory still serves me, Mithras there (in the kingdom of Satan) sets his mark on the foreheads of his soldiers, celebrates also the oblation of bread, and introduces an image of the resurrection, and before a sword wreathes a crown."[1]

Here is another passage:

"Some soldier of Mithras, who at his initiation in the gloomy cavern,—in the camp, it may well be said, of darkness,—when at the sword's point a sword is presented to him as though in mimicry of martyrdom, and thereupon a crown is put upon his head, is admonished to resist and cast it off, and, if you like,

[1] Pres. v., *Hær.* chap. xl.

transfer it to his shoulders, saying that Mithras is his crown. He even has his virgins and his ascetics (*continentes*). Let us take note of the devices of the devil, who is wont to ape some of God's things."[1]

From this it is plain that the worshippers of Mithras had the simple rites of Buddhists and Christians, baptism and the bloodless altar; also an early Freemasonry, which some detect veiled in the Indian life of Buddha. Thus the incident of the sword and crown in the Mithraic initiation is plainly based on the menacing sword of Mâra in the *Lalita Vistara* and the crown that he offered Buddha. In modern Masonry it is feigned that Hiram Abiff, the architect of Solomon's temple, made three efforts to escape from three assassins. These are plainly Old Age, Disease, and Death. He sought to evade the first at the east of the temple, in the same way that Buddha tried to escape by the eastern gate. The second and third flights of Hiram and Buddha were to the same points of the compass. Then Buddha escaped the lower life through the Gate of Benediction, and Hiram was killed. The disciples of Mithras had, in the comedy of their initiation, "seven tortures,"—heat, cold, hunger, thirst, fire, water, etc.,—experiences by no means confined to histrionics in the experience of Buddha's Wanderers. A modern mason goes through the comedy of giving up his gold and silver and baring his breast and feet, a form that once had a meaning. Mithras was born in a cave; and at Easter there was the ceremony called by Tertullian the "image of the resurrection." The worshippers, Fermicus tells us,[2] placed by night a stone

[1] *De Corona*, xv. [2] *De Errore*, xxiii.

image on a bier in a cave and went through the forms of mourning. The dead god was then placed in a tomb, and after a time withdrawn from it. Then lights were lit, and poems of rejoicing sounded out, and the priest comforted the devotees. "You shall have salvation from your sorrows!" Dupuis naturally compares all this to the *cierge pascal* and Catholic rites. In Jerusalem the Greek pontiff goes into the cave called Christ's sepulchre and brings out miraculous fire to the worshippers, who are fighting and biting each other outside, imaging unconsciously Buddha's great battle with Mâra and the legions of hell, its thunder and lightning and turmoil, followed by a bright coruscation, and by the angels who greeted his victory. This sudden illumination, which is the chief rite of Freemasonry, of Mithraism, and of Christianity, has oddly enough been thrown overboard by the English Church.

That Mithraism was at once Freemasonry and Buddhism is proved by its great spread. Buddhism was the first missionary religion. Judaism and the other old priestcrafts were for a "chosen people." At the epoch of Christ, Mithraism had already honeycombed the Roman paganism. Experts have discovered its records in Arthur's Oon and other British caves.

A similar Freemasonry was Pythagoreanism in Greece. Colebrooke, the prince of Orientalists, saw at once that its philosophy was purely Buddhist. Its rites were identical with those of the Mithraists and Essenes. These last must now be considered. They have this importance, that they are due to a separate propagandism. Alexandria was built by the great invader of India, to bridge the East and the West. And an exceptional toleration of creeds was the result.

Neander divides Israel at the date of Christ into three sections:

1. Pharisaism, the "dead theology of the letter."

2. Sadduceeism, "debasing of the spiritual life into worldliness."

3. Essenism, Israel mystical—a "comingling of Judaism with the old Oriental theosophy."

Concerning this latter section, Philo wrote a letter to a man named Hephæstion, of which the following is a portion:

"I am sorry to find you saying that you are not likely to visit Alexandria again. This restless, wicked city can present but few attractions, I grant, to a lover of philosophic quiet. But I cannot commend the extreme to which I see so many hastening. A passion for ascetic seclusion is becoming daily more prevalent among the devout and the thoughtful, whether Jew or Gentile. Yet surely the attempt to combine contemplation and action should not be so soon abandoned. A man ought at least to have evinced some competency for the discharge of the social duties before he abandons them for the divine. First the less, then the greater.

"I have tried the life of the recluse. Solitude brings no escape from spiritual danger. If it closes some avenues of temptation, there are few in whose case it does not open more. Yet the Therapeutæ, a sect similar to the Essenes, with whom you are acquainted, number many among them whose lives are truly exemplary. Their cells are scattered about the region bordering on the farther shore of the Lake Mareotis. The members of either sex live a single and ascetic life, spending their time in fasting and contemplation, in prayer or reading. They believe themselves favoured with divine illumination—an inner light. They assemble on the Sabbath for worship, and listen to mystical discourses on the traditionary lore which they say has been handed down in secret among themselves. They also celebrate solemn dances and processions of a mystic significance by moonlight on the shore of the great mere. Sometimes, on an occasion of public rejoicing, the margin of the lake on our side will be lit with a fiery chain of illuminations, and galleys, hung with lights, row to and fro with strains of music sounding over the broad water. Then the Therapeutæ are all hidden in their little hermitages, and these sights and sounds of the world they have abandoned make them withdraw into themselves and pray.

"Their principle, at least, is true. The soul which is occupied with things above, and is initiated into the mysteries of the Lord, cannot but account the body evil, and even hostile. The soul of man is divine, and his highest wisdom is to become as much as possible a stranger to the body with its embarrassing appetites. God has breathed into man from heaven a portion of His own divinity. That which is divine is invisible. It may be extended, but it is incapable of separation. Consider how vast is the range of our thought over the past and the future, the heavens and the earth. This alliance with an upper world, of which we are conscious, would be impossible were not the soul of man an indivisible portion of that divine and blessed spirit. Contemplation of the divine essence is the noblest exercise of man; it is the only means of attaining to the highest truth and virtue, and therein to behold God is the consummation of our happiness here."

Here we have the higher Buddhism, which seeks to reach the plane of spirit, an "alliance with the upper world" by the aid of solitary reverie. That Philo knew where this religion had come from is, I think, proved by another passage.

"Among the Persians there is the order of Magi who deeply investigate the works of nature for the discovery of truth, and in leisure's quiet are initiated into and expound in clearest significance the divine virtues.

"In India, too, there is the sect of the Gymnosophists, who, in addition to speculative philosophy, diligently cultivate the ethical also, and have made their life an absolute ensample of virtue.

"Palestine, moreover, and Syria are not without their harvest of virtuous excellence, which region is inhabited by no small portion of the very populous nation of the Jews. There are counted amongst them certain ones, by name Essenes, in number about four thousand, who derive their name, in my opinion, by an inaccurate trace from the term in the Greek language for holiness (Essen or Essaios—Hosios, holy), inasmuch as they have shown themselves pre-eminent by devotion to the service of God; not in the sacrifice of living animals, but rather in the determination to make their own minds fit for a holy offering."[1]

Plainly here the Essenes are pronounced of the same

[1] Philo, "Every virtuous man is free."

faith as the Gymnosophists of India, who abstain from the bloody sacrifice, that is the Buddhists.

In the *Revue des Deux Mondes*, 15th July 1888, M. Émile Burnouf has an article entitled "Le Bouddhisme en Occident."

M. Burnouf holds that the Christianity of the Council of Nice was due to a conflict between the Aryan and the Semite, between Buddhism and Mosaism:

"History and comparative mythology are teaching every day more plainly that creeds grow slowly up. None come into the world ready-made, and as if by magic. The origin of events is lost in the infinite. A great Indian poet has said, 'The beginning of things evades us; their end evades us also. We see only the middle.'"

M. Burnouf asserts that the Indian origin of Christianity is no longer contested: "It has been placed in full light by the researches of scholars, and notably English scholars, and by the publication of the original texts. . . . In point of fact, for a long time folks had been struck with the resemblances, or rather the identical elements, contained in Christianity and Buddhism. Writers of the firmest faith and most sincere piety have admitted them. In the last century these analogies were set down to the Nestorians, but since then the science of Oriental chronology has come into being, and proved that Buddha is many years anterior to Nestorius and Jesus. Thus the Nestorian theory had to be given up. But a thing may be posterior to another without proving derivation. So the problem remained unsolved until recently, when the pathway that Buddhism followed was traced step by step from India to Jerusalem."

Another eminent French Orientalist, M. Lêon de Rosny, in a lengthy digest of the present writer's *Influence of Buddhism on Primitive Christianity*, in the *XXme Siècle*, writes with equal conviction:

"The astonishing points of contact (*ressemblances étonnantes*) between the popular legend of Buddha and that of Christ, the almost absolute similarity of the moral lessons given to the world, at five centuries' interval, between these two peerless teachers of the human race, the striking affinities between the customs of the Buddhists and of the Essenes, of whom Christ must have been a disciple, suggest at once an Indian origin to Primitive Christianity."

This raises a great question. I have treated it at length in my *Buddhism in Christendom*, and have little space left. To begin with,—was Jesus an Essene?

Historical questions are sometimes made more clear by being treated broadly. Let us first deal with this from the impersonal side, leaving out altogether the alleged words and deeds of Christ, Paul, etc. Fifty years before Christ's birth there was a sect dwelling in the stony waste where John prepared a people for the Lord. Fifty years after Christ's death there was a sect in the same part of Palestine. The sect that existed fifty years before Christ was called Essenes, Therapeuts, Gnostics, Nazarites. The sect that existed fifty years after Christ's death was called "Essenes or Jesseans" according to Epiphanius, Therapeuts, Gnostics, Nazarites, and not Christians until afterwards.

Each had two prominent rites: baptism, and what Tertullian calls the "oblation of bread." Each had for officers, deacons, presbyters, ephemereuts. Each sect had monks, nuns, celibacy, community of goods. Each interpreted the Old Testament in a mystical way,—so mystical, in fact, that it enabled each to discover that the bloody sacrifice of Mosaism was forbidden, not enjoined. The most minute likenesses have been pointed out between these two sects by all Catholic writers from Eusebius and Origen to the poet Racine, who translated Philo's *Contemplative Life* for the benefit of pious court ladies. Was there any connection between these two sects? It is difficult to conceive that there can be two answers to such a question.

And if it can be proved, as Bishop Lightfoot affirms, that Christ was an anti-Essene, who announced that His mission was to preserve intact every jot and tittle of Mosaism as interpreted by the recognised interpreters, this would simply show that he had nothing to do with the movement to which his name has been given.

The first prominent fact of His life is His baptism by John. If John was an Essene, the full meaning of this may be learnt from Josephus:

"To one that aims at entering their sect, admission is not immediate; but he remains a whole year outside it, and is subjected to their rule of life, being invested with an axe, the girdle aforesaid, and a white garment. Provided that over this space of time he has given proof of his perseverance, he approaches nearer to this course of life, and partakes of the holier water of cleansing; but he is not admitted to their community of life. Following the proof of his strength of control, his moral conduct is tested for two years more; and when he has made clear his worthiness, he is then adjudged to be of their number. But before he touches the common meal, he pledges to them in oaths to make one shudder, first, that he will reverence the Divine Being; and secondly, that he will abide in justice unto men, and will injure no one, either of his own accord or by command, but will always detest the iniquitous, and strive on the side of the righteous; that he will ever show fidelity to all, and most of all to those who are in power, for to no one comes rule without God; and that, if he become a ruler himself, he will never carry insolence into his authority, or outshine those placed under him by dress or any superior adornment; that he will always love truth, and press forward to convict those that tell lies; that he will keep his hands from peculation, and his soul pure from unholy gain; that he will neither conceal anything from the brethren of his order, nor babble to others any of their secrets, even though in the presence of force and at the hazard of his life. In addition to all this, they take oath not to communicate the doctrines to any one in any other way than as imparted to themselves; to abstain from robbery, and to keep close, with equal care, the books of their sect and the names of the angels. Such are the oaths by which they receive those that join them."[1]

As a pendant to this, I will give the early Christian initiation from the Clementine *Homilies*.

"If any one having been tested is found worthy,

[1] Josephus, *De B. J.* ii. 8, 2, 13.

then they hand over to him according to the initiation of Moses, by which he delivered his books to the Seventy who succeeded to his chair."

These books are only to be delivered to "one who is good and religious, and who wishes to teach, and who is circumcised and faithful."

"Wherefore let him be proved not less than six years, and then, according to the initiation of Moses, he (the initiator) should bring him to a river or fountain, which is living water, where the regeneration of the righteous takes place." The novice then calls to witness heaven, earth, water, and air, that he will keep secret the teachings of these holy books, and guard them from falling into profane hands, under the penalty of becoming "accursed, living and dying, and being punished with everlasting punishment."

"After this let him partake of bread and salt with him who commits them to him."

Now, if, as is believed by Dr. Lightfoot, the chief object of Christ's mission was to establish for ever the Mosaism of the bloody altar, and combat the main teaching of the ἀσκητής, or mystic, which "postulates the false principle of the malignity of matter," why did He go to an ἀσκητής to be baptized? Whether or not Christ belonged to mystical Israel, there can be no discussion about the Baptist. He was a Nazarite "separated from his mother's womb," who had induced a whole "people" to come out to the desert and adopt the Essene rites and their community of goods. And we see, from a comparison of the Essene and early Christian initiations, what such baptism carried with it. It implied preliminary instruction and vows of implicit obedience to the instructor.

It is plain too that the Essene Christ knows at first nothing of any antagonism to His teacher.

"The law and the prophets were until John. Since that time the kingdom of God is preached, and every man presseth into it" (Luke xvi. 16).

This shows that far from believing that He had come to preserve the Mosaism of the bloody altar, He considered that John and the Essenes had power to abrogate it.

Listen, too, to Christ's instructions to his twelve disciples:

"As ye go, preach, saying the kingdom of heaven is at hand."

This is the simple gospel of John:

"Provide neither gold nor silver nor brass in your purses, nor scrip for your journey, neither two coats, neither shoes."

Here again we have the barefooted Essenes without silver or gold. "He that hath two coats let him impart to him that hath none," said the Baptist. "And into whatsoever city or town ye shall enter, inquire who in it is worthy; and there abide till ye go thence. And when ye come into an house, salute it. And if the house be worthy, let your peace come upon it; but if it be not worthy, let your peace return to you. And whosoever shall not receive you, nor hear your words, when ye depart out of that house or city, shake off the dust of your feet. Verily I say unto you, It shall be more tolerable for the land of Sodom and Gomorrha in the day of judgment, than for that city. Behold, I send you forth as sheep in the midst of wolves: be ye therefore wise as serpents, and harmless as doves. But beware of men; for they will deliver you up to the councils, and they will scourge you in their synagogues; and ye shall be brought before governors and kings for my sake, for a testimony against them and the Gentiles. But when they deliver you up, take no thought how or what ye shall speak; for it shall be given you in that same hour what ye shall speak. For it is not ye that speak, but the Spirit of your Father which speaketh in you. And the brother shall deliver up the brother to death, and the father the child: and the children shall rise up against their parents, and cause them to be put to death. And ye shall be hated of all men for my name's sake: but he that endureth to the end shall be saved."

This passage is remarkable. No Christian disciple had yet begun to preach, and yet what do we find? A vast secret organisation in every city. It is composed of those who are "worthy" (the word used by Josephus for Essene initiates); and they are plainly bound to succour the brethren at the risk of their lives. This shows that Christ's movement was affiliated with an earlier propagandism.

There is another question. On the hypothesis that Christ was an orthodox Jew, why should He, plainly knowing beforehand what mistakes and bloodshed it would cause, make His disciples mimic the Essenes in externals? The Essenes had two main rites, baptism and the bloodless oblation. Christ adopted them. The Essenes had a new name on conversion.

"Thou shalt be called Cephas, which is, by interpretation, a stone" (John i. 42).

The Essenes had community of goods:

"And all that believed were together, and had all things common" (Acts ii. 44).

"If thou wilt be perfect, go and sell that thou hast, and give to the poor, and thou shalt have treasure in heaven; and come and follow me" (Matt. xix. 21).

A rigid continence was exacted:

"All men cannot receive this saying, save they to whom it is given. . . . There be eunuchs which have made themselves eunuchs for the kingdom of heaven's sake. He that is able to receive it, let him receive it" (Matt. xix. 11, 12).

"And I looked, and, lo! a Lamb stood on Mount Zion, and with him an hundred and forty-four thousand, having his Father's name written on their foreheads. . . . These are they which were not defiled with women, for they are virgins" (Rev. xiv. 1, 4).

Divines tell us that this first passage is to have only a "spiritual" interpretation. It forbids not marriage, but excess. We might listen to this if we had not historical cognisance of a sect in Palestine at this date which enforced celibacy in its monasteries. The second passage shows that the disciples understood Him literally.

The bloody sacrifice forbidden:

"I will have mercy and not sacrifice" (Matt. ix. 13).

"Unless ye cease from sacrificing, the wrath shall not cease from you."[1]

Bishop Lightfoot, as I have mentioned, considers that Jesus was an orthodox Jew, whose mission was to perpetuate every jot and tittle of Mosaism; and that "emancipation" from the "swathing-bands" of

[1] Cited from Gospel of the Hebrews by Epiphanius, *Hær.* xxx. 16.

the law came from the Apostles.[1] It might be thought that this was a quaint undertaking for the Maker of the million million starry systems to come to this insignificant planet in bodily form to "perpetuate" institutions that Titus in thirty years was to end for ever; even if we could forget that human sacrifices, concubinage, polygamy, slavery, and border raids were amongst these institutions. But if this Christ is the historical Christ, it appears to me that we must eliminate the Christ of the Gospels almost entirely. For capital offences against the Mosaic law, the recognised authorities three times sought the life of Jesus, twice after formal condemnation by the Sanhedrim. These offences were Sabbath-breaking, witchcraft, and speaking against Mosaic institutions. According to the Synoptics, He never went to Jerusalem during His ministry until just the end of it; although the three visits for the yearly festivals were rigidly exacted.

In my *Buddhism in Christendom* I give reasons for supposing that the "multitudes," whose sudden appearance in stony wastes have bewildered critics, were in reality the gatherings for the Therapeut festivals described by Philo.

Bishop Lightfoot makes much of the fact that John's Gospel makes Christ go up once for the feast of tabernacles. But did He go as an orthodox worshipper, to present His offerings for the bloody sacrifice? On the contrary, on this very occasion He was accused of Sabbath-breaking and demoniac possession; and the rulers of the people sent officers to arrest Him.

[1] *Com. on Galatians*, pp. 286, 287.

It must be mentioned, too, that Hegesippus, the earliest Christian historian, gives a very remarkable picture of James, who ruled the Christian body after Christ's death: "He was consecrated from his mother's womb. He drank neither wine nor strong drink, neither ate he any living thing. A razor never went upon his head. He anointed not himself with oil, nor did he use a bath. He alone was allowed to enter into the holies. For he did not wear woollen garments, but linen. And he alone entered the sanctuary and was found upon his knees praying for the forgiveness of the people, so that his knees became hard like a camel's through his constant bending and supplication before God, and asking for forgiveness for the people."[1]

Here we have the chief apostle depicted as an Essene of Essenes. He rejects wine and flesh meat. And the "temple" of the Essenes was plainly not the Jewish temple. The temple guards would have made short work of any one rash enough to attempt to enter the Holy of Holies.

Epiphanius adds the two sons of Zebedee to the list of the ascetics, and also announces that James, the chief apostle, entered the Holy of Holies once a year. He gives another detail, that the Christian bishop wore the bactreum or metal plate of the high priest.[2]

Clement of Alexandria gives a similar account of St. Matthew.

"It is far better to be happy than to have a demon dwelling in us. And happiness is found in the practice of virtue. Accordingly, the Apostle Matthew partook of seeds, and nuts, and vegetables without flesh."[3]

[1] Eusebius, *Hist. Eccl.* ii. 33. [2] Epiph. *Hær.* lxxviii. 13, 41.
[3] *Pædag.* ii. 1.

The Clementine *Homilies* give a far more authentic picture of the Church of Jerusalem than the Acts. In them St. Peter thus describes himself:

"The Prophet of the Truth who appeared on earth taught us that the Maker and God of all gave two kingdoms to two (beings), good and evil, granting to the evil the sovereignty over the present world. . . Those men who choose the present have power to be rich, to revel in luxury, to indulge in pleasures, and to do whatever they can; for they will possess none of the future goods. But those who have determined to accept the blessings of the future reign have no right to regard as their own the things that are here since they belong to a foreign king, with the exception only of water and bread and those things procured with sweat to maintain life (for it is not lawful to commit suicide); and also only one garment, for they are not permitted to go naked."[1]

A word here about the *Sepher Toldoth Jeshu*, a work which orthodoxy as usual would modernise overmuch. It is a brief sketch of Christ's life, and at any rate represents the Jewish tradition of that important event. It announces that the Saviour was hanged on a tree for sorcery. After that there was a bitter strife between the "Nazarenes" and the "Judeans." The former, headed by Simon Ben Kepha (who, "according to his precept," abstained from all food, and only ate "the bread of misery" and drank the "water of sorrow"), altered all the dates of the Jewish festivals to make them fit in with events in Christ's life. This seems to make Peter and the "Nazarenes" or Nazarites water-drinking vegetarian ascetics.

[1] Clem. *Hom.* xv. 7.

CHAPTER X

MORE COINCIDENCES

I HAVE shown certain curious points of contact between the Buddhist and the Christian scriptures. Here are a few more.

"THEN WAS JESUS LED UP BY THE SPIRIT INTO THE WILDERNESS, TO BE TEMPTED OF THE DEVIL"

Comfortable dowagers driving to church three times on Sunday would be astonished to learn that the essence of Christianity is in this passage. Its meaning has quite passed away from Protestantism, almost from Christendom. The *Lalita Vistara* fully shows what that meaning is. Without Buddhism it would be lost. Jesus was an Essene, and the Essene, like the Indian Yogi, sought to obtain divine union and the "gifts of the Spirit" by solitary reverie in retired spots. In what is called the "Monastery of our Lord" on the Quarantania, a cell is shown with rude frescoes of Jesus and Satan. There, according to tradition, the demoniac hauntings that all mystics speak of occurred.

"I HAVE NEED TO BE BAPTIZED OF THEE"

A novice in Yoga has a guru, or teacher. Buddha, in riding away from the palace, by and by reached a jungle near Vaiśâlî. He at once put himself under a Brahmin Yogi named Arâta Kâlâma, but his spiritual insight developed so rapidly that in a short time the Yogi offered to Buddha the arghya, the offering of rice, flowers, sesamun, etc., that the humble novice usually presents to his instructor, and asked him to teach instead of learning.[1]

Thirty Years of Age

M. Ernest de Bunsen, in his work, *The Angel Messiah*, says that Buddha, like Christ, commenced preaching at thirty years of age. He certainly must have preached at Vaiśâlî, for five young men became his disciples there, and exhorted him to go on with his teaching.[2] He was twenty-nine when he left the palace, therefore he might well have preached at thirty. He did not turn the wheel of the law until after a six years' meditation under the Tree of Knowledge.

Baptism

The Buddhist rite of baptism finds its sanction in two incidents in the Buddhist scriptures. In the first, Buddha bathes in the holy river, and Mâra, the evil spirit, tries to prevent him from emerging. In the second, angels administer the holy rite (Abhisheka).

"And when He had fasted Forty Days and Forty Nights"

Buddha, immediately previous to his great encounter with Mâra, the tempter, fasted forty-nine days and nights.[3]

[1] Foucaux, *Lalita Vistara*, p. 228.
[2] *Lalita Vistara*, p. 236.
[3] *Chinese Life*, by Wung Puh.

"Command that these Stones be made Bread"

The first temptation of Buddha, when Mâra assailed him, appealed to his hunger, as we have seen.

The twelve great Disciples

"Except in my religion, the twelve great disciples are not to be found."[1]

"The Disciple whom Jesus loved"

One disciple was called Upatishya (the beloved disciple). In a former existence he and Maudgalyâyana had prayed that they might sit, the one on the right hand and the other on the left. Buddha granted this prayer. The other disciples murmured much.[2]

"Go ye into all the World"

From Benares Buddha sent forth the sixty-one disciples. "Go ye forth," he said, "and preach Dharma, no two disciples going the same way."[3]

"The Same came to Jesus by Night"

Professor Rhys Davids points out that Yâsas, a young rich man, came to Buddha by night for fear of his rich relations.

Pax Vobiscum

On one point I have been a little puzzled. The password of the Buddhist Wanderers was Sadhu! which does not seem to correspond with the "Pax

[1] Bigandet, p. 301. [2] *Ibid.* p. 153. [3] *Ibid.* p. 126.

Vobiscum!" (Matt. x. 13) of Christ's disciples. But I have just come across a passage in Renan[1] which shows that the Hebrew word was Schalom! (*bonheur!*). This is almost a literal translation of Sadhu!

Burnouf says that by preaching and miracle Buddha's religion was established. In point of fact, it was the first universal religion. He invented the preacher and the missionary.

"A NEW COMMANDMENT GIVE I YOU, THAT YE LOVE ONE ANOTHER"

"By love alone can we conquer wrath. By good alone can we conquer evil. The whole world dreads violence. All men tremble in the presence of death. Do to others that which ye would have them do to you. Kill not. Cause no death."[2]

THE BEATITUDES

The Buddhists, like the Christians, have got their Beatitudes. They are plainly arranged for chant and response in the temples. It is to be noted that the Christian Beatitudes were a portion of the early Christian ritual.

The "long suffering and meek," those "who follow a peaceful calling," those who are not "weary in well-doing" are included in the catalogue.

Here is one verse:

"10 *Self-restraint* and *purity*,
The knowledge of noble truths,
The attainment of Nirvâṇa,—
This is the greatest blessing."

---

[1] *Les Apôtres*, p. 22.

[2] "Sûtra of Forty-two Sections," v. 129.

The One Thing needful

Certain subtle questions were proposed to Buddha, such as: What will best conquer the evil passions of man? What is the most savoury gift for the alms-bowl of the mendicant? Where is true happiness to be found? Buddha replied to them all with one word, *Dharma* (the heavenly life).[1]

"Whosoever shall smite thee on thy Right Cheek offer him the Other also"

A merchant from Sûnaparanta having joined Buddha's society, was desirous of preaching to his relations, and is said to have asked the permission of the master so to do.

"The people of Sûnaparanta," said Buddha, "are exceedingly violent; if they revile you, what will you do?"

"I will make no reply," said the mendicant.

"And if they strike you?"

"I will not strike in return," said the mendicant.

"And if they kill you?"

"Death," said the missionary, "is no evil in itself. Many even desire it to escape from the vanities of life."[2]

Buddha's Third Commandment

"Commit no adultery." Commentary by Buddha: "This law is broken by even looking at the wife of another with a lustful mind."[3]

[1] Bigandet, p. 225. [2] *Ibid.* p. 216.
[3] Buddhaghosa's *Parables*, by Max Müller and Rodgers, p. 153.

The Sower

It is recorded that Buddha once stood beside the ploughman Kasibhâradvaja, who reproved him for his idleness. Buddha answered thus: "I, too, plough and sow, and from my ploughing and sowing I reap immortal fruit. My field is religion. The weeds that I pluck up are the passions of cleaving to this life. My plough is wisdom, my seed purity."[1]

On another occasion he described almsgiving as being like "good seed sown on a good soil that yields an abundance of fruits. But alms given to those who are yet under the tyrannical yoke of the passions are like a seed deposited in a bad soil. The passions of the receiver of the alms choke, as it were, the growth of merits."[2]

"Not that which goeth into the Mouth defileth a Man"

In the *Sutta Nipâta* (chap. ii.) is a discourse on the food that defiles a man (Âmaghanda). Therein it is explained at some length that the food that is eaten cannot defile a man, but "destroying living beings, killing, cutting, binding, stealing, falsehood, adultery, evil thoughts, murder"—this defiles a man, not the eating of flesh.

"Where your Treasure is"

"A man," says Buddha, "buries a treasure in a deep pit, which lying concealed therein day after day profits him nothing, but there is a treasure of charity, piety,

[1] *Hardy Manual*, p. 215. [2] Bigandet, p. 211.

temperance, soberness, a treasure secure, impregnable, that cannot pass away, a treasure that no thief can steal. Let the wise man practise Dharma. This is a treasure that follows him after death."[1]

The House on the Sand

"It [the seen world] is like a city of sand. Its foundation cannot endure."[2]

Blind Guides

"Who is not freed cannot free others. The blind cannot guide in the way."[3]

"As ye sow, so shall ye reap"

"As men sow, thus shall they reap."[4]

"A Cup of cold Water to one of these little Ones"

"Whosoever piously bestows a little water shall receive an ocean in return."[5]

"Be not weary in Well-Doing"

"Not to be weary in well-doing."[6]

"Give to him that asketh"

"Give to him that asketh, even though it be but a little."[7]

[1] *Khuddaka Pâtha*, p. 13.
[2] *Lalita Vistara*, p. 172.
[3] *Ibid.* p. 179.
[4] *Ta-chwang-yan-king-lun*, serm. 57.
[5] *Ibid.* serm. 20.
[6] *Mahâmangala Sutta*, ver. 7.
[7] *Udânavarga*, chap. xx. ver. 15.

"Do unto Others," etc.

"With pure thoughts and fulness of love I will do towards others what I do for myself."[1]

"Prepare ye the Way of the Lord!"

"Buddha's triumphant entry into Râjâgṛiha (the "City of the King") has been compared to Christ's entry into Jerusalem. Both, probably, never occurred, and only symbolise the advent of a Divine Being to earth. It is recorded in the Buddhist scriptures that on these occasions a "Precursor of Buddha" always appears.[2]

"Who did sin, this Man or his Parents, that he was born Blind?" (John ix. 3)

Professor Kellogg, in his work entitled *The Light of Asia and the Light of the World*, condemns Buddhism in nearly all its tenets. But he is especially emphatic in the matter of the metempsychosis. The poor and hopeless Buddhist has to begin again and again "the weary round of birth and death," whilst the righteous Christians go at once into life eternal.

Now, it seems to me that this is an example of the danger of contrasting two historical characters when we have a strong sympathy for the one and a strong prejudice against the other. Professor Kellogg has conjured up a Jesus with nineteenth century ideas, and a Buddha who is made responsible for all the fancies that were in the world B.C. 500. Professor

[1] *Lalita Vistara*, chap. v.

[2] Bigandet, p. 147.

Kellogg is a professor of an American university, and as such must know that the doctrine of the *gilgal* (the Jewish name for the metempsychosis) was as universal in Palestine A.D. 30, as it was in Râjâgṛiha B.C. 500. An able writer in the *Church Quarterly Review*, of October 1885, maintains that the Jews brought it from Babylon. Dr. Ginsburg, in his work on the "Kabbalah," shows that the doctrine continued to be held by Jews as late as the ninth century of our era. He shows, too, that St. Jerome has recorded that it was "propounded amongst the early Christians as an esoteric and traditional doctrine."

The author of the article in the *Church Quarterly Review*, in proof of its existence, adduces the question put by the disciples of Christ in reference to the man that was born blind. And if it was considered that a man could be born blind as a punishment for sin, that sin must have been plainly committed before his birth. Oddly enough, in the *White Lotus of Dharma* there is an account of the healing of a blind man, "Because of the sinful conduct of the man [in a former birth] this malady has risen."

But a still more striking instance is given in the case of the man sick with the palsy (Luke v. 18). The Jews believed, with modern Orientals, that grave diseases like paralysis were due, not to physical causes in this life, but to moral causes in previous lives. And if the account of the cure of the paralytic is to be considered historical, it is quite clear that this was Christ's idea when He cured the man, for He distinctly announced that the cure was effected not by any physical processes, but by annulling the "sins" which were the cause of his malady.

Traces of the metempsychosis idea still exist in Catholic Christianity. The doctrine of original sin is said by some writers to be a modification of it. Certainly the fancy that the works of supererogation of their saints can be transferred to others is the Buddhist idea of good karma, which is transferable in a similar manner.

"If the Blind lead the Blind, both shall fall into the Ditch" (Matt. xv. 14)

"As when a string of blind men are clinging one to the other, neither can the foremost see, nor the middle one see, nor the hindmost see. Just so, methinks, Vâsettha is the talk of the Brahmins versed in the Three Vedas."[1]

"Eunuchs for the Kingdom of Heaven's Sake"

In the days of St. Thomas à Kempis the worshipper was modelled on the Christ. In our days the Christ seems modelled on the worshipper. The Bodleian professor of Sanskrit writes thus: "Christianity teaches that in the highest form of life love is intensified; Buddhism teaches that in the highest state of existence all love is extinguished. According to Christianity—Go and earn your own bread, and support yourself and your family. Marriage, it says, is honourable and undefiled, and married life a field where holiness can grow."

But history is history; and a French writer has recently attacked Christ for attempting to bring into Europe the celibacy and pessimism of Buddhism.

[1] Buddha, in the *Tevigga Sutta*, i. 15.

This author in his work, *Jésus Bouddha,* cites Luke xiv. 26:

"If any man come to Me, and hate not his father, and mother, and *wife,* and children, and brethren, and sisters, yea, and his own life also, he cannot be My disciple."

He adduces also:

"Let the dead bury their dead.

"Think not that I have come to send peace on earth: I come not to send peace, but a sword. For I am come to set a man at variance against his father, and the daughter against her mother, and the daughter-in-law against her mother-in-law. And a man's foes shall be they of his own household" (Matt. x. 34–36).

"And the brother shall deliver up the brother to death, and the father the child; and the children shall rise up against their parents, and cause them to be put to death" (*Ibid.* ver. 21).

"So likewise, whosoever he be of you that forsaketh not all that he hath, he cannot be my disciple" (Luke xiv. 33).

The author says that all this is pure nihilism, and Essene communism. "The most sacred family ties are to be renounced, and man to lose his individuality and become a unit in a vast scheme to overturn the institutions of his country."

"Qu' importe au fanatisme la ruine de la société humaine."

Here also is a remarkable passage from an American writer:

"The anticosmic tendency of the Christian doctrine," says Mr. Felix Oswald,[1] "distinguishes it from all

[1] *Secret of the East,* p. 27.

religions except Buddhism. In the language of the New Testament the 'world' is everywhere a synonym of evil and sin, the flesh everywhere the enemy of the spirit. . . . The gospel of Buddha, though pernicious, is, however, a perfectly consistent doctrine. Birth, life, and re-birth is an eternal round of sorrow and disappointment. The present and the future are but the upper and lower tire of an ever-rolling wheel of woe. The only salvation from the wheel of life is an escape to the peace of Nirvâṇa. The attempt to graft this doctrine upon the optimistic theism of Palestine has made the Christian ethics inconsistent and contradictory. A paternal Jehovah, who yet eternally and horribly tortures a vast plurality of his children. An earth the perfect work of a benevolent God, yet a vale of tears not made to be enjoyed, but only to be despised and renounced. An omnipotent heaven, and yet unable to prevent the intrigues and constant victories of hell. Christianity is evidently not a homogeneous but a composite, a hybrid religion; and considered in connection with the indications of history, and the evidence of the above-named ethical and traditional analogies, these facts leave no reasonable doubt that the founder of the Galilean Church was a disciple of Buddha Śâkya muni" (p. 139).

All this is very well if the Buddhists by "salvation" meant escape from life, and not from sin. A "pessimist" Buddhist kingdom, according to this, ought to present the universal sad faces of the "Camelot" of a modern school of artists, and yet the Burmese are pronounced by all to be the merriest and happiest of God's creatures. We know, too, that

India never was so prosperous as in the days of Buddhist rule. The monks carried agriculture to high perfection; and Indian fabrics were famous everywhere. A convent meant less a career than an education in spiritual knowledge. Like the Essene, the Buddhist monk was not forced to remain for life. Catholicism introduced that change.

"Then all His Disciples forsook Him and fled"

It is recorded that on one occasion when a "must" elephant charged furiously, "all the disciples deserted Buddha. Ânanda alone remained."[1]

"If thy right Eye offend thee."

Mr. Felix Oswald[2] announces, without, however, giving a more detailed reference, that according to Max Müller's translation of the "Ocean of Worlds," a young monk meets a rich woman who pities his hard lot.

"Blessed is the woman who looks into thy lovely eyes!"

"Lovely!" replied the monk. "Look here!" And plucking out one of his eyes he held it up, bleeding and ghastly, and asked her to correct her opinion.

Walking on the Water

Certain villagers, hard of belief, were listening to Buddha on the shore of a mighty river. Suddenly by a miracle the great teacher caused a man to appear walking on the water from the other side, without immersing his feet.[3]

[1] *Fo-sho-hing-tsan-king*, iv. 21. [2] *The Secret of the East*, p. 134.
[3] *Chinese Dhammapada*, p. 51.

"AND, LO! THERE WAS A GREAT CALM"

Pûrna, one of Buddha's disciples, had a brother in danger of shipwreck in a "black storm." But the guardian spirits of Pûrna informed him of this. He at once transported himself through the air from the distant inland town to the deck of the ship. "Immediately the black tempest ceased as if Sumeru had arrested it."[1]

"WHY EATETH YOUR MASTER WITH PUBLICANS AND SINNERS?" (Matt. ix. 10)

The courtesan Amrapalî invited Buddha and his disciples to a banquet in the mango grove at Vaiśâlî. Buddha accepted. Some rich princes, sparkling in emeralds, came and gave him a similar invitation. He refused. They were very angry to see him sit at meat with Amrapalî. He explained to his disciples that the harlot might enter the kingdom of Dharma more easily than the prince.[2]

THE PENITENT THIEF

Buddha confronts a terrible bandit in his mountain retreat and converts him.[3]

"THERE WAS WAR IN HEAVEN"

Professor Beal, in his *Catena of Buddhist Scriptures* (p. 52), tells us that, in the *Saddharma Prâ-*

[1] Burnouf, Introd. p. 229.
[2] Bigandet, p. 251.
[3] *Chinese Dhammapada*, p. 98.

kasa Sasana Sûtra, a great war in heaven is described. In it the "wicked dragons" assault the legions of heaven. After a terrific conflict they are driven down by Indra and the heavenly hosts.

"THE KINGDOM OF HEAVEN IS LIKE UNTO A MERCHANTMAN SEEKING GOODLY PEARLS, WHO, WHEN HE HAD FOUND ONE PEARL OF GREAT PRICE, WENT AND SOLD ALL THAT HE HAD AND BOUGHT IT" (Matt. xiii. 45)

The most sacred emblem of Buddhism is called the maṇi (pearl), and in the Chinese biography a merchant-man seeking goodly pearls finds it, and unfortunately drops it into the sea. Rather than lose it he tries to drain the sea dry.[1]

THE VOICE FROM THE SKY

This sounds often in the Buddhist narratives.[2]

FAITH

"Faith is the first gate of the Law."[3]

"All who have faith in me obtain a mighty joy."[4]

"THOU ART NOT YET FIFTY YEARS OLD, AND HAST THOU SEEN ABRAHAM?"

In the *White Lotus of Dharma* (chap. xiv.) Buddha is asked how it is that, having sat under the bo-tree only forty years ago, he has been able, according to

[1] *Rom. Hist.* p. 228.
[2] See Beal, *Rom Hist.* p. 105.
[3] *Lalita Vistara*, p. 39.
[4] *Ibid.* p. 188.

his boast, to see many Buddhas and saints who died hundreds of years previously. He answers that he has lived many hundred thousand myriads of Kotis, and that though in the form of a Buddha, he is in reality Swayambhu, the Self-Existent, the Father of the million worlds. In proof of this statement he causes two Buddhas of the Past, Prabhûtaratna and Gadgadesvara, to appear in the sky. The first pronounces loudly these words: "It is well! It is well!" These Buddhas appear with their sepulchral canopies (stûpas) of diamonds, red pearls, emeralds, etc. Peter, at the scene of the Transfiguration, said to Christ:

"Let us make here three tabernacles—one for Thee, one for Moses, and one for Elias." Why should Peter want to adopt a Buddhist custom and build tabernacles for the dead Moses and the dead Elias? Why, also, should Moses come from the tomb to support a teacher who had torn his covenant with Yahve to shreds?

"He was transfigured before them"

Buddha, leaving Maudgalyâyana and another disciple to represent him, went off through the air to the Devaloca, to the Heaven Tuśita, to preach to the spirits in prison and to convert his mother. When he came down from the mountain (Mienmo), a staircase of glittering diamonds, seen by all, helped his descent. His appearance was blinding. The "six glories" glittered on his person. Mortals and spirits hymned the benign Being who emptied the hells.[1]

In the Gospel according to the Hebrews is a curious

[1] Bigandet, p. 209.

passage, which Baur and Hilgenfeld hold to be the earliest version of the Transfiguration narrative.

"Just now my mother, the Holy Spirit, took me by one of my hairs and bore me up on to the great mountain of Tabor."

This is curious. Buddha and Jesus reach the Mount of Transfiguration, each through the influence of his mother. But perhaps the Jewish writer did not like the universalism inculcated in the Buddhist narrative.

"He began to wash the Disciples' Feet" (John xiii. 5)

In a vihâra at Gândhâra was a monk so loathsome and stinking, on account of his maladies, that none of his brother disciples dare go near him. The great Teacher came and tended him lovingly and washed his feet.[1]

The great Banquet of Buddha

In the *Lalita Vistara* (p. 51) it is stated that those who have faith will become "sons of Buddha," and partake of the "food of the kingdom." Four things draw disciples to his banquet—gifts, soft words, production of benefits, conformity of benefits.

Baptism

In a Chinese life of Buddha by Wung Puh,[2] it is announced that Buddha at Vaiśâlî delivered a Sûtra

[1] *Chinese Dhammapada*, p. 94.

[2] See Beal, *Journ. As. Soc.* vol. xx. p. 172.

entitled, "The Baptism that Rescues from Life and Death and Confers Salvation."

"And none of them is lost but the Son of Perdition"

Buddha had also a treacherous disciple, Devadatta. He schemed with a wicked prince, who sent men armed with bows and swords to slaughter Buddha. Devadatta tried other infamous stratagems. His end was appalling. Coming in a palanquin to arrest Buddha, he got out to stretch himself. Suddenly fierce flames burst out, and he was carried down to the hell Avîchi (the Rayless Place). There, in a red-hot cauldron, impaled by one red bar and pierced by two others, he will stay for a whole Kalpa. Then he will be forgiven.[1]

The Last Supper

Buddha had his last supper or repast with his disciples. A treacherous disciple changed his alms-bowl, and apparently he was poisoned.[2] Fierce pains seized him as he journeyed afterwards. He was forced to rest. He sent a message to his host, Kunda, the son of the jeweller, to feel no remorse although the feast had been his death. Under two trees he now died.

It will be remembered that during the last supper of Jesus a treacherous disciple "dipped into his dish," but as Jesus was not poisoned, the event had no sequence.

[1] Bigandet, p. 244. [2] See Rockhill's *Buddha*, p. 133.

"Now from the Sixth Hour there was Darkness over all the Land until the Ninth Hour"

The critical school base much of their contention that the Gospels do not record real history on this particular passage. They urge that such an astounding event could not have escaped Josephus and Tacitus. When Buddha died, the "sun and moon withdrew their shining," and dust and ashes fell like rain. "The great earth quaked throughout. The crash of the thunder shook the heavens and the earth, rolling along the mountains and valleys."[1] The Buddhist account is certainly not impossible, for the chronicler takes advantage of the phenomena of an Indian dust-storm to produce his dark picture. At Lucknow, before the siege, I remember a storm so dense at midday that some ladies with my regiment thought the Day of Judgment had arrived.

"And many Bodies of the Saints which slept arose"

When Buddha died at Kuśinagara, Ânanda and another disciple saw many denizens of the unseen world in the city, by the river Yigdan.[2]

"To anoint My Body to the Burying" (Mark xiv. 8)

The newly discovered fragments of the Gospel of Peter give us a curious fact. They record that Mary

[1] *Fo-sho-hing-tsan-king*, v. 26.
[2] Rockhill's *Life of the Buddha*, p. 133.

Magdalene, "taking with her her friends," went to the sepulchre of Jesus to "place themselves beside him and perform the rites" of wailing, beating breasts, etc. Amrapalî and other courtesans did the same rites to Buddha, and the disciples were afterwards indignant that impure women should have "washed his dead body with their tears."[1]

In the Christian records are three passages, all due, I think, to the Buddhist narrative. In one, "a woman" anoints Jesus; in John (xii. 7), "Mary" anoints him; in Luke, a "sinner," who kisses and washes his feet with her hair. Plainly these last passages are quite irrational. No woman could have performed the washing and other burial rites on a man alive and in health.

"They parted My Garments"

The Abbé Huc tells us[2] that on the death of the Bokté Lama his garments are cut into little stripes and prized immensely.

"He appeared unto Many"

Buddha prophesied that he would appear after his death.[3] In a Chinese version quoted by Eitel,[4] Buddha, to soothe his mother, who had come down weeping from the skies, opens his coffin lid and appears to her. In the temple sculptures he is constantly depicted coming down to the altar during worship.[5]

[1] Rockhill, *Thibetan Life*, p. 153.
[2] *Voyages*, ii. p. 278.
[3] *Lotus*, p. 144.
[4] *Three Lectures*, p. 57.
[5] See illustrations to my *Buddhism in Christendom*.

The "Great White Throne"

Mr. Upham, in his *History of Buddhism* (pp. 56, 57), gives a description of the Buddhist heaven. There is a "high mountain," and a city "four square" with gates of gold and silver, adorned with precious stones. Seven moats surround the city. Beyond the last one is a row of marble pillars studded with jewels. The great throne of the god stands in the centre of a great hall, and is surmounted by a white canopy. Round the great throne are seated heavenly ministers, who record men's actions in a "golden book." A mighty tree is conspicuous in the garden. In the Chinese heaven is the "Gem Lake," by which stands the peach-tree whose fruit gives immortality.

The Atonement

The idea of transferred good Karma, the merits of the former lives of an individual being passed on to another individual, is, of course, quite foreign to the lower Judaism, which believed in no after life at all. In the view of the higher Buddhism, Śâkya Muni saved the world by his teaching; but to the lower, the Buddhism of offerings and temples and monks, this doctrine of Karma was the life-blood. It was proclaimed that Buddha had a vast stock of superfluous Karma, and that offerings at a temple might cause the worshipper in his next life to be a prince instead of a pig or a coolie. In the *Lalita Vistara*[1] it is announced that when Buddha overcame Mâra, all flesh rejoiced, the blind saw, the deaf heard, the dumb

[1] Chinese version, p. 225.

spake, the hells were cleared, and all by reason of Buddha's Karma in previous lives.

St. Paul is very contradictory about the atonement. This passage seems pure Buddhism:

"As by the offence of one judgment came upon all men to condemnation, even so by the righteousness of one the free gift came upon all men unto justification of life" (Rom. v. 18).

Contrast this with another passage:

"Whom God hath set forth to be a propitiation, through faith in His blood, to declare His righteousness for the remission of sins" (Rom. iii. 25).

CHAPTER XI

RITES

I HAVE left myself little space to write of the many points of close similarity between the Buddhists and the Roman Catholics.

The French missionary Huc, in his celebrated travels in Thibet, was much struck with this similarity.

"The crozier, the mitre, the dalmatic, the cope or *pluvial*, which the grand lamas wear on a journey, or when they perform some ceremony outside the temple, the service with a double choir, psalmody, exorcisms, the censer swinging on five chains and contrived to be opened and shut at will, benediction by the lamas, with the right hand extended over the heads of the faithful, the chaplet, sacerdotal celibacy, Lenten retirements from the world, the worship of saints, fasts, processions, litanies, holy water—these are the points of contact between the Buddhists and ourselves."

Listen also to Father Disderi, who visited Thibet in the year 1714. "The lamas have a tonsure like our priests, and are bound over to perpetual celibacy. They study their scriptures in a language and in characters that differ from the ordinary characters. They recite prayers in choir. They serve the temple, present the offerings, and keep the lamps perpetually alight. They offer to God corn and barley and paste and water in little vases, which are extremely clean. Food thus offered is considered consecrated, and they eat it. The lamas have local superiors, and a superior general."[1]

Father Grueber, with another priest, named Dorville, passed from Pekin through Thibet to Patna in the year 1661. Henry Prinsep[2] thus sums up what he has recorded:

"Father Grueber was much struck with the extraordinary similarity he found, as well in the doctrine as in the rituals of the Buddhists of Lha Sa, to those of his own Romish faith. He noticed, first, that the dress of the lamas corresponded to that handed down to us in ancient paintings as the dress of the Apostles. Second, that the discipline of the monasteries and of the different orders of lamas or priests bore the same resemblance to that of the Romish Church. Third, that the notion of an Incarnation was common to both, so also the belief in paradise and purgatory. Fourth, he remarked that they made suffrages, alms, prayers, and sacrifices for the dead, like the Roman Catholics. Fifth, that they had convents filled with monks and friars to the number of thirty thousand, near Lha Sa, who all made the three vows of poverty, obedience, and chastity, like Roman monks, besides other vows. Sixth, that they had confessors licensed by the superior lamas or bishops, and so empowered to receive confessions, impose penances, and give absolution. Besides all this there was found the practice of using holy water, of singing service in alternation, of

[1] *Lettres Édifiantes*, vol. iii. p. 534.

[2] *Thibet Tartary, etc.* p. 14.

praying for the dead, and of perfect similarity in the customs of the great and superior lamas to those of the different orders of the Romish hierarchy. These early missionaries further were led to conclude, from what they saw and heard, that the ancient books of the lamas contained traces of the Christian religion, which must, they thought, have been preached in Thibet in the time of the Apostles."

In the year 1829 Victor Jacquemont, the French botanist, made a short excursion from Simla into Thibet. He writes: "The Grand Lâma of Kanum has the episcopal mitre and crozier. He is dressed just like our bishops. A superficial observer at a little distance would take his Thibetan and Buddhist mass for a Roman mass of the first water. He makes twenty genuflexions at the right intervals, turns to the altar and then to the congregation, rings a bell, drinks in a chalice water poured out by an acolyte, intones paternosters quite of the right sing-song—the resemblance is really shocking. But men whose faith is properly robust will see here nothing but a corruption of Christianity." [1]

It must be borne in mind that what is called Southern Buddhism has the same rites. St. Francis Xavier in Japan found Southern Buddhism so like his own that he donned the yellow *sanghâti*, and called himself an apostle of Buddha, quieting his conscience by furtively mumbling a little Latin of the baptismal service over some of his "converts."

This is what the Rev. S. Beal, a chaplain in the navy, wrote of a liturgy that he found in China:

[1] *Corr.* vol. i. p. 265.

"The form of this office is a very curious one. It bears a singular likeness in its outline to the common type of the Eastern Christian liturgies. That is to say, there is a 'Proanaphoral' and an 'Anaphoral' portion. There is a prayer of entrance (τῆς εἰσοδου), a prayer of incense (τοῦ θυμιάματος), an ascription of praise to the threefold object of worship (τρισαγίον), a prayer of oblation (τῆς προσ θεσεως), the lections, the recitations of the Dharanî (μυστηριον), the Embolismus, or prayer against temptation, followed by a 'Confession' and a 'Dismissal.'"[1]

Turning to architecture, I must point out that Mr. Ferguson, the leading authority in ancient art, was of opinion that the various details of the early Christian basilica—nave, aisle, columns, semi-domed apse, cruciform ground plan—were borrowed *en bloc* from the Buddhists. Mr. Ferguson lays special stress on the Dâgoba and its enshrined relics, represented in the Christian Church by the high altar, the bones of a saint, the baldechino. Relic-worship, he says, was certainly borrowed from the East. Of the rock-cut temple of Kârle (B.C. 78) he writes:

"The building resembles, to a great extent, an early Christian Church in its arrangements, consisting of a nave and side aisles terminating in an apse or semi-dome, round which the aisle is carried. . . . As a scale for comparison, it may be mentioned that its arrangements and dimensions are very similar to those of the choir of Norwich Cathedral, and of the Abbaye aux Hommes at Caen, omitting the outer aisles in the latter buildings.

"Immediately under the semi-dome of the apse, and

[1] *Catena of Buddhist Scriptures*, p. 397.

nearly where the altar stands in Christian Churches, is placed the Dâgoba.[1]"

The list of resemblances is by no means exhausted. The monks on entering a temple make the gesture that we call the sign of the cross. The Buddhists have illuminated missals, Gregorian chants, a tabernacle on the altar for oblations, a pope, cardinals, angels with wings, saints with the nimbus. For a full account I must refer the reader to my *Buddhism in Christendom*, where I give (pp. 182, 184) drawings of monks and nuns, the Virgin and Child (p. 205), the adoration of the rice cake on the altar (p. 83), Buddha coming down to the altar with the heavenly host (p. 210), the long candles, artificial flowers, cross, incense burner, and divine figure with the aureole, of the Buddhist temple (p. 208). The election of the Grand Lâma I show to be pin for pin like the election of the Pope. The list is endless.

How is all this to be accounted for? Several theories have been started:

The first attempts to make light of the matter altogether. All religions, it says, have sacrifice, incense, priests, the idea of faith, etc. This may be called the orthodox Protestant theory, and many bulky books have recently appeared propounding it. But as these books avoid all the strong points of the case, they cannot be called at all satisfactory to the bewildered inquirer.

To this theory the Roman Catholics reply that the similarities between Buddhism and Catholicism are so microscopic and so complete, that one religion must have borrowed from the other. In consequence they

[1] *Indian and Eastern Architecture*, p. 117.

try to prove that the rites of Buddhism and the life of its founder were derived from Christianity, from the Nestorians, from St. Thomas, from St. Hyacinth of Poland, from St. Oderic of Frioul.[1]

In the way of this theory, however, there are also insuperable difficulties. Buddha died 470 years before Christ, and for many years the Christian Church had no basilicas, popes, cardinals, basilica worship, nor even for a long time a definite life of the founder. At the date of Aśoka (B.C. 260) there was a metrical life of Buddha (Muni Gâtha), and the incidents of this life are found sculptured in marble on the gateways of Buddhist temples that precede the Christian epoch. This is the testimony of Sir Alexander Cunningham, the greatest of Indian archæologists. He fixes the date of the Bharhut Stûpa at from 270 to 250 B.C. There he finds Queen Mâyâ's dream of the elephant, the Ṛishis at the ploughing match, the transfiguration of Buddha and the ladder of diamonds, and other incidents. At the Sanchi tope, an earlier structure (although the present marble gateways, repeated probably from wood, are fixed at about A.D 19), he announces representations of Buddha as an elephant coming down to his mother's womb, three out of the "Four Presaging Tokens," Buddha bending the bow of Sinhahanu, King Bimbisâra visiting the young prince, and other incidents.

A man who invents, let us say, a submarine boat, at once puts his idea to a practical test. Let us try and construct a working model here. Suppose that the present ruler of Afghanistan were paying us a visit, and, introduced at Fulham Palace, he were to suggest

[1] See Abbé Prouvéze, *Life of Gabriel Durand*, vol. ii. p. 365.

that the life of Mahomet should supersede that of Jesus in our Bible, and Mussulman rites replace the Christian ritual in the diocese of London. What would be the answer? The bishop, anxious to deal gently with a valuable ally, would point out that he was only a cogwheel in a vast machinery, a cogwheel that could be promptly replaced if it proved the least out of gear. He would show that the Anglican Church had a mass of very definite rules called canon law, with courts empowered to punish the slightest infringement of these rules. He would show that even an archbishop could not alter a tittle of the gospel narrative. Every man, woman, and child would immediately detect the change.

Similar difficulties would be in the way of St. Hyacinth of Poland in, say, a monastery of Ceylon. The abbot there would be responsible to what Bishop Bigandet calls his "provincial," and he again to his "supérieur général" (p. 478), and so on to the Âchârya, the "High Priest of all the World," who, in his palace at Nalanda, near Buddha Gayâ, was wont to sit in state, surrounded by ten thousand monks. Buddhism, by the time that a Christian missionary could have reached it, was a far more diffused and conservative religion than Anglicanism. It had a canon law quite as definite. It had hundreds of volumes treating of the minutest acts of Śâkya Muni.

CHAPTER XII

BUDDHA IN NORWAY AND AMERICA

NORWAY

ONE portion of Her Majesty's subjects calls the fourth day of the week the "Day of Woden," and a still larger portion calls it the "Day of Buddha." Is there any connection between Woden and Buddha? Professor Max Müller ridicules the idea; on the other hand, the great archæologist, Professor Holmboe, takes up the opposite view. In the first place, the earliest traditions of the Norsemen and their earliest historians assert that they came from beyond the Tanaqvisl (Don or Tanais), from Asaland, from the city of Asgard; and these Asas are identified by the professor as the Asioi or Asiani of Strabo and other classical writers, certain invaders of Bactria from beyond the Jaxartes. These Asas arrived in Norway, and they have left behind them an abundance of monuments which prove that their rites, and temples, and symbols are precisely the same as those of the Buddhists. The haug is a servile copy of the tope; and its concomitants, the stambha or solitary tower, the circles of upright stones, the tank or lake for baptismal purposes, and the sacred trees, are everywhere found. Inside these haugs are discovered copies of the coins of Bactrian kings of the first century A.D., and also many Buddhist symbols—the Swastica, the Nandâvarta, and the professor might have added, as I shall show, the Triratna. To make his case more complete, the professor points to a line of these haugs and circles stretching across Europe, which indicates the pathway of these migrating Asas; and the *w* and *b* in Sanskrit being identical letters, the word Woden, he points out, could have easily been manufactured out of Bodhi, Budh, etc.

A rough heap or cairn of stones was the primitive idea of the tope. In the tope *par excellence* the hemispherical shape was adopted as the most complete representation of the heaven of the Buddhists. The tope at Sanchi, near Bhilsâ, in Bhopal, is a simple hemisphere, and was erected about the middle of the sixth century B.C., according to General Cunningham. The next oldest topes are the smaller Bhilsâ topes. In these the hemisphere is raised up a few feet by the addition of a cylindrical portion. In the Afghan topes, which were erected about the Christian era, the hemisphere is still farther elevated. In a fourth class of tope, of which the Sârnâth tope at Benares is a fine specimen, the cylindrical portion is as high as the diameter of the tope.

In India the origin of the tope is attributed to Buddha; in Norway the haug is attributed to Woden. Snorro Sturlasen, in his *History of the Ancient Kings of Norway*, thus writes: "Woden gave to the kingdom the law which governs tho Asas. He ordered that all the dead should be burned, and their property should be carried with them to the pyre. In this way each would reach Walhalla with his riches; he would enjoy also all that he had hid in the earth. The ashes were to be thrown in the sea or buried."

Let us now compare the haug and the tope.

"The tumuli of Europe," says the professor, "composed of stones, sand, and earth, have received the most natural shape for a heap, that of a truncated cone rounded at the top. The topes of Asia developed gradually from the earliest cuneiform stûpa or heap, which was replaced, to get the inner cell more solid, by a quadrangular wall surmounted by a cone. Then this construction was raised aloft from its base by a cylinder. The haugs of Norway and the topes of Asia seem to have had originally the same form, and the sole difference between these ancient monuments is the more developed form of the topes, which have, however, always retained the conic cupola, striking a mean between the cone and the hemisphere. In Norway and Tibet square monuments of the same description are found, although these are exceptional. "Also, in Norway we find tumuli with a little tumulus at the summit of each, as if to imitate the topes with their basement, which in Afghanistan is more often a heap of stones thrown together without order. In Jutland and at Bornholm are tumuli of this construction."

Another point of resemblance traced by the professor is the immense masses of materials heaped up to produce an imposing effect. The Valders haug at Valderoe, an island belonging to Norway, is four hundred feet in circumference, and must have been once about thirty feet high. Another haug, the Ous Haug, is four hundred and fifty feet in circumference; a haug at Yttre Holmedel is four hundred feet in circumference. Turning to the topes, we find that the Amarâvati is five hundred feet in circumference, and now about sixteen feet high. This is about the height of most of the

Norwegian haugs. The Bhilsâ tope is five hundred and fifty-four feet in circumference. The Manikyala tope, between Attock and Lahore, is three hundred and twenty feet in circumference. The haugs are constructed without the use of cement; with this exception, says the professor, a "more faithful imitation of the Eastern construction was quite impossible."

When we examine the interior of the monuments, the similarity continues. Topes are usually built up by the aid of more than one cupola. A small cupola is constructed, and then a larger one outside that, the intervening space being filled up with rough stones. Within the smaller cupola are sometimes found smaller cupolas of metal (gold, silver, and copper), the one within the other, boxes holding probably relics and other precious treasures. This custom of making use of more than one cupola is also peculiar to the haug. One at Ostreim, in the diocese of Bergheim, is made up of three or four cupolas roughly built, the intermediate space being filled in with rubble and turf, with coal, and then with more layers of rubble and turf, and then more coal. In the parish of Urland, in the parish of Lekanger, in the parish of Haus, haugs with interior cupolas of similar construction have been found.

In the centre of both tope and haug is a quadrangular cell formed of flags of stone at a level with or just above the basement. Narrow horizontal passages sometimes connect these with the outside.

In their accessories the tope and the haug have fresh points of similarity. Above the haug is often found a monolith pointed at the top. This reminds the professor of the spires of the topes, and, indeed, was plainly the Ch'attra. Then, again, imitations of the tope railing, imperfect, no doubt, from want of the power of working in stone, have been attempted in Norway, notably at the Kongs haug at Karmöe. Ranges of cells are found, too, in both tope and haug. Ditches are often found round both. Tanks, ponds, lakes, holy water of some sort, must be near these sacred edifices. The famous circles of upright monoliths are also found near them.

"The articles deposited in the topes and the haugs are almost the same. In the inner cells of the topes fine raked mould is found, or sand and cinders, forming often a compact mass. In some topes nothing else has been found; in others, beneath this mass of earth were urns or vases containing earth of a reddish colour, mingled with ochre. Sometimes in these urns were found human ashes and fragments of bones, and sometimes, in addition, coins and ornaments. These vases are of gold, silver, copper, or iron. In one case a wooden vase has been discovered. Many of these vases, the one within the other, and the most precious one in the centre, are found in the same cell. The ornaments were deposited sometimes in the vase itself, sometimes in the surrounding earth; and these ornaments consisted of pearls, precious stones, rings, golden bells, and other gold objects of various shapes, gold leaf, silver rings, etc. In the matter of glass and crystal, a few cylinders have been found, and two little phials, one of which was upset and had its cork alongside. It contained a few drops of fluid. In a silver vase a fluid was also found, brown and of pungent smell. Resinous and fatty matter has also been found in some of the topes, and fragments of bark and leaves. Once the bark had been made into a box. Oval and spherical stones have also been discovered.

"Having thus enumerated the principal objects that have been found in the topes, let us glance at the contents of the haugs. Their cells also contain fine mould (mixed sometimes with red sand and ochre), formed into a concrete mass. Urns or vases have also been discovered, in iron and copper, in wire and in wood. Glass vases have also been found. These vases, of which several have been discovered in the same cell, contain human ashes, fragments of gold, ornaments, gold coins, etc. The ornaments consist of pearls, brooches, rings, etc., in gold, silver, and bronze; specimens of gold and gold leaf, fatty and resinous matter, fragments of wood and bark, and a box made of the bark of a tree, have also been discovered. One bell has been found, and also, in a glass vase, some drops of a fluid, brown and pungent. Once a phial was found also having traces of fluid. The coins, with one exception, are all in gold; the exception was a silver coin."

In the topes, lamps are found; in the haugs, never,—although in the cells of the latter there are traces of smoke. In connection with both topes and haugs are traditions of phantom coruscations seen at night, which the professor connects with the lamps burning inside. Sacred trees and groves are near both topes and haugs whenever practicable. The vihâras (convents) in Norway were built of wood, and have disappeared, but some traces of them still remain. In Norway the arms of the faithful were frequently deposited in the haugs, but the tope builders always bore in mind that the great Buddha detested such things.

Let us sum up the results already established by Professor Holmboe:—

1. In Norway and the other haunts of the Norsemen

are found five religious erections and their concomitants—the tumulus, the broch, the circle of stones, the tank, and the oval sepulchral hill, which five institutions belong to Buddha, and no other known faith.

2. The Asas profess to have come from Asaland and Asgard, beyond the Tanais, regions which from about B.C. 200 were Buddhist.

3. This history is confirmed by a line of circles and tumuli, indicating their passage across Europe to Scandinavia.

But it is when we turn from monuments to mythology that our difficulties begin. Iceland has preserved for us a rich crop of those myths in the "Elder" and "Younger" Eddas. And in these we cannot fail to see at once a faith radically differing from Buddhism. As in the Bhagavad Gîtâ, the courage of the hero is apparently the first of virtues. Abundant flesh of the boar Sæhrimmer will keep him happy after death, and many flagons of celestial beer poured out by the Valkyries. But then it might be urged by Professor Holmboe that the migratory race that transferred Indra and his Apsarases to Norway might also have brought the Indian creed that upset India. The most splendid haug in Norway is the Valders' haug, the Tumulus of Balder,—and Balder is a gentle god, peaceful, forgiving, in fact, quite out of touch with the boosy, fighting Norse gods and men. Then, too, in Norse records it is announced that Leif, son of Erick the Red, visited Vinland A.D. 1000. If Vinland is America, as is now believed, and if in America there are found any traces of Buddhism, the case of Professor Holmboe would of course be stronger.

BUDDHA IN AMERICA

The popular notion that Columbus and his followers were the first inhabitants of the Eastern hemisphere that reached the Western continent is becoming dissipated by modern research. M. A. de Quatrefages maintains that the discovery of the black man, the white man, and the yellow man amongst the so-called aborigines is a proof of the distinct migrations of each of those great human families. He shows that there are many points where geography would assist migrations by sea. At Behring Straits the two continents are brought close together, and the passage is partly bridged by the group of the St. Laurence Islands. Kamtschatka and Alaska, with the intervening Aleutian Islands, show another point of passage in the Polar regions which the Tchukchees on both shores frequently use. The currents of Tessan, the Black Stream of the Japanese, have frequently cast floating bodies and abandoned junks upon the shores of California. The equatorial current of the Atlantic opens a similar route, leading from Africa to America.

The Chinese books speak of a country called Fou Sang, to which they sent Buddhist missionaries in the fifth century. Fou Sang is 20,000 li (a li is 486 yards) from China. In following the course of the Black Stream of the Japanese, these figures would bring us to California, where the abandoned junks were stranded. Fou Sang means literally, the extreme east.

Klaproth has combated the idea that Fou Sang is the continent of America, and holds that it meant Japan. But M. de Risny has shown from a Japanese encyclopædia that the Japanese also were aware of these Buddhist missions to a distant land, which they call Fou So. The Chinese writers speak of copper, gold, and silver being found in Fou Sang, but no iron. This description applies to America, but not to Japan. M. Paravey gives a Chinese drawing of the American llama in one of his books. "I have heard M. Castelnau say," says M. de Quatrefages, "'When I was surrounded by my Siamese servants, I imagined myself in America!'" In the *Geografia del Peru*, by Paz Soldan, it is asserted that Chinese recently brought to the province of Lambayéque were able to converse with the American natives. In the large folio designs, furnished by the Abbé Brasseur de Bourbourg, is one large head so boldly painted that it might well have been one of the Japanese embassy painted by a modern artist. Pearl fishery, and the employment of murex for its beautiful purple dye, are other points which show the teaching of some Eastern nation.

Humboldt and Laplace have detected points of similarity between the astronomy of the Mexicans and that of the Old World far too striking to be the result of mere chance. The Mexicans had the twenty-eight mansions of the lunar zodiac, which, as I have shown, is far more ancient than the solar zodiac of twelve mansions. Humboldt also was much struck with the similarity between the symbols of the Mexican zodiac and those of the Buddhist Tartars. He pointed out that the Mexicans have "nine lords of the night," corresponding to the "nine astrological signs of several nations of Asia" (the seven planets and the two great serpents). The number nine, he asserts, was plainly chosen because it divides into the 360 days of the lunar year.

"The intercalation of twenty-five days in one hundred and four years," says Laplace, "supposes a more exact duration of the tropical years than that of Hipparchus, and, what is very remarkable, almost equal to that of the astronomers of Almamon. When we consider the difficulty of attaining so exact determination we are led to believe that it is not the work of the Mexicans, and that it reached them from the old continent."

It is to be mentioned that in the Mexican zodiac are the ass and the tiger, not indigenous in America, the serpent, the horse, and what is of immense importance, the Makara (cipactli) of Buddhism.

Also they have everywhere the topes and standing-stones, and the serpent-symbols of the Buddhists, and a tradition of Quatzalcoatl, who forbade human and other bloody sacrifices, and substituted offerings of flowers.

The Mexicans had the Buddhist rite of baptism. The Mexicans had the Buddhist bloodless oblation, which took the form of little images of maize dough. They had processions, a hierarchy, religious communities, periods of penance. They had secret mysteries, divided into three grades of initiation. They had the sign of the cross, also the mystic vase. They had a tradition of a flood, and of the escape of one man. In their narrative of the deluge was also the incident of the dove. The priests of Cortes saw in all this Satan parodying the mysteries of Christianity. Even the intelligent Abbé Guerin, in India, was convinced that the Institutes of Manu were plagiarised from the Latin vulgate. Regarding the rewards and punishments of the future, ideas analogous to those of the Buddhists were found in the New World.

"Those who have gone to the regions of punishment, they believe to be tortured for a time proportioned to the amount of their transgressions, and that they are then to be transferred to the land of the happy, where they are again liable to the temptations of the evil spirit, and answerable again at a future period for their new offences."

They held also that the world was supported on a great tortoise, which animal was one of the most holy of their emblems.

But the best proof of Buddhist proselytism is found in the pictures and statues of the Mexican Buddha. He is called Xaca, which word M. Paravey plausibly identifies with Śâkya. These can be seen in the designs furnished by the Abbé Brasseur de Bourbourg from Palenqué. M. Paravey showed Burnouf one of these Buddhas without telling him where it had been found. The great Sanskrit scholar at once pronounced it to be a representation of Śâkya Muni.

I have only been able to touch on these great questions, not to solve them. How it is that the propagandism of the Buddhist missionaries has been so successful, and the work of other missionaries so fruitless, would be an interesting inquiry. To this rule there is one exception—the missionary labours of the higher Christianity before it was tainted and stiffened by contact with the lower.

CHAPTER XIII

CONCLUSION

Dr. Crozier, in the *Fortnightly Review* for February 1899, is very hostile to Buddhism and the Indian religions. He announces that "thought in its evolution will no more return to them than the animal kingdom will return to the marsupials." The Indian God, he holds, is an "impotent" God. He is described as a "Great Soul," and modern thought requires a God with will and energy, a God who can, in fact, look after the world. The Indian Gods discountenance action and work on behalf of our fellow-men, and lead their devotees to occupy themselves mainly in saving their own souls" by "thinking of this Supreme Soul when in a state of ecstasy, the eyes being fixed on the tip of the nose."

This deserves attention. The Indian philosophers have no doubt always been a little vague about their God. This is done purposely. They say that if you begin to limit the Absolute it becomes the Absolute no longer. "Un Dieu defini," says the French wit, "c'est un Dieu fini!"

The East clings to symbols, to metaphor. They break their God to pieces and make his attributes into little Gods. The West loves a God that—what shall I say?—can be photographed. "From his *tapas*," says a Buddhist book, speaking of the Buddha of Buddhas, "the universe was produced by him. He is the Iswara (Creator), the infinite, the form of all things yet formless."

Here we are in the presence of two ideas that elucidate one another. In India the *Ṛishi*, the magician, was said to perform his magical acts when in *tapas*, the mystical, magical trance. Hence the Buddha of Buddhas and the Brahmin Gods are imaged in what Dr. Crozier calls "a state of ecstasy, the eyes being fixed on the tip of the nose," and if Brahma created evolution and then sate still, he really seems quite as much up to modern thought as, say, Paley's watchmaker God who goes about correcting the works of his not quite perfect watches. But this Indian symbolism goes much deeper. The enlightened man and the enlightening God have the same symbolic representation, because in a sense they are one.

"What is God?" said the missionary Robson to a Brahmin:

"He is talking to you."

There lies the distinction between the East and the West. The God of the West is outside humanity. The God of the East is sought for in the human breast.

But in justice to Dr. Crozier, we may mention that the modern, up-to-date philosophers fare as badly at his hands as the marsupial Gods of India. He cites a speech uttered by Carlyle when he called upon that great sage in Chelsea. "We have reached the comfortable conclusion that God is a myth, that the soul is gas, and the next world a coffin." As a substitute for all this, Dr. Crozier gives us a philosophy of his own.

He calls it the "Scale in the Mind." In every one of us is a sort of "Judge." He is "in the mind," but "not of the mind." He is neither "conscience, honour, beauty, reverence, nor love." He is a sort, in fact, of subliminal Baron Hawkins, and he tells even the higher animals when they are doing wrong.[1] But is all this getting rid of the marsupial Brahma, or bringing him back again in a horse-hair wig?

There are differences between the two Brahmas, but is the balance of merits with Dr. Crozier's Brahma? The King of Benin, when his favourite wife has the *tic douloureux*, believes that Mumbo Jumbo is angry because he has broken some silly law of the Taboo. At once inspired by his remorse or his "Scale in the Mind," he orders the massacre of fifty subjects to appease the deity. Does not this give us the difference between Dr. Crozier's and the Indian Brahma. The first is ready to inspire anybody; the second must have the mind prepared and the soul purified before he can enter.

One chief popular objection to Buddhism runs after this fashion. "It is much better that a respectable young man should toil and till, and marry and raise up a healthy family, than abandon his young wife like Buddha and sit idly under a tree.

This is true; but if the Indian philosophers had not reasoned and reflected in solitude, there would probably still be nothing to till, and the respectable young man would have to share his wife with the rest of the village or, perhaps, monkey gang. The philosopher's work was at first utilitarian, as well as superstitious. He fashioned bows and arrows, as well as imprecations. He designed rude strategy and rude politics. He superintended agriculture. He invented rude moral codes.

Three main points are urged by Dr. Crozier against Buddha:

[1] Crozier, *My Inner Life*, p. 433.

1. He discountenanced work and action on behalf of our fellow-men.

2. He urged folks to save their own souls by contemplation and asceticism.

3. Buddhism had no support in its system for a doctrine of love.[1]

I will write down a few of the achievements of this inactive Buddha and the army of *Bhikshus* that he directed:

1. The most formidable priestly tyranny that the world had ever seen crumbled away before his attack, and the followers of Buddha were paramount in India for a thousand years.

2. The institution of caste was assailed and overturned.

3. Polygamy was for the first time pronounced immoral, and slavery condemned.

4. Woman, from being considered a chattel and a beast of burden, was for the first time considered man's equal, and allowed to develop her spiritual life.

5. All bloodshed, whether with the knife of the priest or the sword of the conqueror, was rigidly forbidden.

6. Also, for the first time in the religious history of mankind, the awakening of the spiritual life of the individual was substituted for religion by body corporate. It is also certain that Buddha was the first to proclaim that duty was to be sought in the eternal principles of morality and justice, and not in animal sacrifices and local formalities invented by the fancy of priests.

7. The principle of religious propagandism was for the first time introduced with its two great instruments, the missionary and the preacher.

[1] *Fortnightly Review*, February 1899

8. By these, India, China, Bactria, and Japan, were proselytised; and the Buddhist missionaries overran Persia and Egypt. This success was effected by moral means alone, for Buddhism is the one religion guiltless of coercion. It is reckoned that one-third of humanity is still in its fold.

9. Without entering any further into the great question of what Christ added to or what Christ removed from Essenism, it is plain that from Buddha came the main elements that changed Mosaism into the leading creed of Europe.

10. One great gift of Buddha to the world is quite overlooked. In the Institutes of Manu are noted down all sorts of penalties for the heretics who question the Brahmin claims. We know, too, that Plato was sold as a slave for his opinions, and Socrates put to death. Buddhism is the religion of the individual, and from the first it seems to have held toleration of other creeds as a logical outcome. A few years ago an English officer in Ceylon, in civil employ, gained the affections of his district. At his death the Buddhists came forward and offered to build an English church as a memorial. In India during the one thousand years of Buddhist rule all creeds and all philosophies were tolerated, a priceless and unexampled boon to the thought of the world.

The second contention of Dr. Crozier is that Buddhism is pure selfishness; and the third, that Buddha had no idea of love, whereas Jesus by His sacrifice saved the world.

A clever Buddhist answered the missionaries a few years ago in a little work called *Happiness*, and in his view the selfishness and absence of love and charity were to be found in quite a different direction. This anonymous Buddhist affirmed that the God of the Christians was chiefly an object to be feared. He lived in a remote "heaven" listening to perpetual songs of praise. He was a "jealous God" ready to consign almost all His creatures to perpetual torment, including "800,000,000 Buddhists in every fifty years," as the author was assured by a missionary. This God proclaimed that credulity and subserviency to His priests was the supreme human merit, and that independent thought, reason, philosophy, and soul dreams, the great sins. His motto was, "The fear of God is the beginning of wisdom."

Upon this statement the writer pounced with much vivacity. There was an Ego and a non-Ego, and this non-Ego was God. He was not in a remote heaven but here on earth, and the one object of the Buddhist was to sink the Ego and its petty dreams and become in harmony with the Supreme Mind. With the Buddhist the fear of the Ego was the beginning of wisdom; not the fear of the non-Ego, which was wisdom itself.

I do not think it does much good to compare Buddhism and Christianity under their modern aspects, and to argue from these that Jesus taught this and Buddha that. The house of Aaron kept the "key" of the great Temple of "Knowledge," with its hopes and dreams. They refused to go in themselves, and "them that were entering they hindered" (Luke xi. 52). Buddha likewise found a mischievous hereditary priesthood, and his great work, like that of Jesus, was to democratise religion. His special characteristic as an epoch-maker I conceive to be this, that he devised less a teaching than an apparatus for spreading a teaching. His famished, half-naked *Parivrâjikas* marched everywhere, taught everywhere, openly if possible, secretly if necessary. Their secret societies, Mithraists, Hermetists, Pythagoreans, and the guardians of the Kabbalah (a treatise of palpable Buddhist inspiration) soon spread over all Europe and Asia Minor. They faced, undaunted, Rome (Christian and un-Christian), the Moslem, the Inquisition. The achievements of the Mussulman Society of the Rose and the persecuted "Kabbalists" read like a fairy tale. The Reformation and the great French Revolution are attributed to them by the enthusiastic followers of St. Martin and the Illuminati.

Men have lived in the past whom Plato or Clement of Alexandria would have praised. Men have lived in the past (a distinct group) whom John Stuart Mill or Professor Clifford would have praised. Would these last writers have given Buddha a place amongst the world's epoch-makers?

Sir Alexander Cunningham, whose knowledge (and love) of old India was unique amongst moderns, announces[1] that Aśoka was the first monarch to bring the whole of India under control of a vigorous and consolidated government. He broke up the smaller States, the little nests of brigands. For war, over an area bigger than Europe, he substituted peace; for border raids, commerce; for the hereditary pretensions of the Brahmins, the claims of individual conscience and reason. His *Dharmsâlas* were hostelries, hospitals, secular schools, as well as convenient spots for mystical dreamers. They were advanced posts for

[1] *Bhilsa Topes*, p. 98.

man in his great struggle with the potent forces of nature, for the engineer, the feller of forests, the drainer of swamps, the sinker of wells, the maker of roads. From Buddhist rule soon emerged a prosperity never known in India before or since. Vast cities surged up with domes that defy the centuries, with delicate carvings, with rock-cut temples. Pataliputra (the modern Patna) stretched for nine miles along the Ganges and for a mile and a half inland. Kapilavastu, Buddha's birthplace, is said to have been of the same vast proportions. Râjâgṛiha was an enormous city. Nalanda, the Rome of the Buddhist hierarchy, accommodated thirty thousand monks. From the great city of Besnagur for a score of miles stretches a range still called the "Mountain of Shrines" (*Chaityagiri*). It was crowded with monasteries, topes, buildings, including the great Sanchi temple.

"The presence of these large monastic establishments must, for a time at least, have brought both wealth and prosperity to the country; and the remains of their embankments thrown across the valleys between Sanchi and Satdhâra show that the Buddhist monks were as famous for practical agriculture as for philosophical learning."[1]

And Buddha's undaunted *Parivrâjikas* carried peace and civilisation across the seas as well as through the jangals. Aśoka himself sent his son Mahendra to Ceylon, and that island was promptly converted to the Buddhist faith. At a later date Java was gained over, a fact testified by its fine Buddhist temples and sculptures. Buddhism invaded Japan, Burmah, Cathay. Sumatra is the Sanskrit

[1] Cunningham, *Bhilsa Topes*, p. 365.

word Samudra. Socotra is also claimed by Sanskrit scholars. Professor Gustav Oppert, in his *Ancient Commerce of India*, shows that Indian merchants were settled in Alexandria, and that a statue in honour of the river Indus was set up there. A valuable work has come down to us, entitled *The Circumnavigation of the Indian Ocean*. It is attributed by Dr. Hunter[1] to a merchant who wrote about A.D. 80, the palmy days of Indian Buddhism. The work gives a "wonderfully complete presentment of the Indo-Egyptian trade," and a list of ninety-five of the chief articles of the traffic. Pliny regrets that fifty-five million sesterces (£458,000) were annually drained from the West to go to the East. A Chinese book of botany ascribed to a prefect of Canton mentions plants growing there in the fourth century A.D. which seem to have been brought by traders from Arabia and the Roman provinces. The "knif-cash" of China have been traced to the Indian Ocean, if we may trust the late M. Terrien de la Couperie, prince of sinologists.

How much of this material prosperity was due to lay energy and how much to Buddha and his monks it is impossible now to settle. Cunningham holds that the Buddhist, like the Roman hierarchy, made and unmade kings. In the days of Fa Hian, the Chinese traveller (A.D. 400), the proudest monarchs "took off their tiaras in the presence of the monks." "All the learning, all the wealth, was in the hands of the Bhikshus." It has always struck me that we have never heard the whole story of Aśoka's conversion from Brahminism to Buddhism. If the Buddhist

[1] *History of India*, vol. i. p. 42.

monks of India worked their propagandism in the form of a secret society, as they undoubtedly did at a very early date in Persia, in Egypt, in Palestine, it is possible that the good king was in the first instance a shrewd politician, and that his hands were forced.

Majestic and calm amid the overturned priestly tyrannies that his *Dharma* has compassed sits the great figure of Buddha, careless alike of idolatry and misrepresentation. That this unique man is entitled to a niche in the great Pantheon of the World's Epoch-Makers scarcely admits of a question.

GLOSSARY AND INDEX

Yoga (lit. "union"), the conjoining of heaven and earth, spirit, and matter, the annihilation of the ego and merging of one's will with the divine will. Magical powers were conceived to be a result of this "union." Hence Yoga also means white magic.

THE WORLD'S EPOCH-MAKERS.

EDITED BY

OLIPHANT SMEATON.

MESSRS. CHARLES SCRIBNER'S SONS have much pleasure in announcing an important new Series, under the title of

"THE WORLD'S EPOCH-MAKERS."

The Volumes composing it will constitute, when their issue is complete, a valuable conspectus of the origin and progress of the most prominent movements that have taken place in theology, philosophy, and the history of intellectual development from Buddha to the present day.

Each Volume will record the initiation and trace the Evolution of some particular phase of human thought and culture. The various subjects have in every case been assigned to writers who have made a special study of them. The Publishers, therefore, confidently expect that the successive Volumes will present the latest and most reliable information on the topics whereon they treat, and that the Series as a whole will be found to afford a valuable guide to the consecutive study of the leading Epochs in the moral, intellectual, and spiritual development of humanity.

For List of Volumes see following pages.

*

THE WORLD'S EPOCH-MAKERS.

BUDDHA AND BUDDHISM.
The First Bursting of the Fetters of Ignorance and Superstition. By ARTHUR LILLIE, M.A., London. [*Now ready.*

SOCRATES.
The Moral Awakening of the Western World. By Rev. J. T. FORBES, M.A., Edinburgh.

PLATO AND ARISTOTLE.
A Contrast and Appreciation. By Professor D. G. RITCHIE, M.A., University of St. Andrews.

MARCUS AURELIUS AND THE LATER STOICS.
The Last and the Greatest Age of Stoicism. By F. W. BUSSELL, D.D., Vice-Principal of Brasenose College, Oxford.

ORIGEN AND GREEK PATRISTIC THEOLOGY.
By Rev. W. FAIRWEATHER, M.A.

AUGUSTINE AND LATIN PATRISTIC THEOLOGY.
By Professor B. B. WARFIELD, D.D., Princeton.

MAHOMET AND MAHOMETANISM.
By P. DE LACY JOHNSTONE, M.A.(Oxon.).

ANSELM AND *CUR DEUS HOMO.*
By Rev. A. C. WELCH, B.D.

FRANCIS AND DOMINIC—THE FOUNDERS OF THE MENDICANT ORDERS.
Monasticism and its Reform. By Professor J. HERKLESS, D.D., University of St. Andrews.

SCOTUS ERIGENA AND HIS EPOCH.
By R. LATTA, Ph.D., D.Sc., University College, Dundee.

WYCLIF AND THE LOLLARDS.
By Rev. J. C. CARRICK, B.D.

THE MEDICI AND THE ITALIAN RENAISSANCE.
By OLIPHANT SMEATON, M.A., Edinburgh.

THE TWO BACONS AND EXPERIMENTAL SCIENCE.
Showing how ROGER BACON prepared the way for FRANCIS BACON, LORD VERULAM. By Rev. W. J. COUPER, M.A.

SAVONAROLA.
By G. M'HARDY, D.D.

LUTHER AND THE GERMAN REFORMATION.
By Professor T. M. LINDSAY, D.D., F.C. College, Glasgow. [*Now ready.*

CRANMER AND THE ENGLISH REFORMATION.
By A. D. INNES, M.A.(Oxon.), London. [*Now ready.*

CALVIN AND THE REFORMED THEOLOGY.
By Principal SALMOND, D.D., F.C. College, Aberdeen.

PASCAL AND THE PORT ROYALISTS.
By Professor W. CLARK, LL.D., D.C.L., Trinity College, Toronto.

DESCARTES, SPINOZA, AND THE NEW PHILOSOPHY.
By Professor J. IVERACH, D.D., F.C. College, Aberdeen.

THE HERSCHELS.
By JAMES SIME, M.A.

WESLEY AND METHODISM.
By F. J. SNELL, M.A.(Oxon.). [*Now ready.*

LESSING AND THE NEW HUMANISM.
Including Baumgarten and the Science of Æsthetics. By Rev. A. P. DAVIDSON, M.A.

HUME AND HIS INFLUENCE ON PHILOSOPHY AND THEOLOGY.
By Professor J. ORR, D.D., Edinburgh.

ROUSSEAU AND NATURALISM IN LIFE AND THOUGHT.
By Professor W. H. HUDSON, M.A., Leland Stanford Junior University, California.

KANT AND HIS PHILOSOPHICAL REVOLUTION.
By Professor R. M. WENLEY, D.Sc., Ph.D., University of Michigan.

SCHLEIERMACHER AND THE REJUVENESCENCE OF THEOLOGY.
By Professor A. MARTIN, D.D., New College, Edinburgh.

HEGEL AND HEGELIANISM.
By Professor R. MACKINTOSH, D.D., Lancashire Independent College, Manchester.

NEWMAN AND HIS INFLUENCE.
By C. SAROLEA, Ph.D., Litt. Doc., University of Edinburgh.

NEW YORK: CHARLES SCRIBNER'S SONS.